1/11
X2

STAY
IN
YOUR
LANE

STAY IN YOUR LANE

Judge Karen's Guide to Living Your Best Life

JUDGE KAREN MILLS-FRANCIS

in collaboration with
Roy L. Brunson and Veronica Mills-Raymond

 ONE WORLD   BALLANTINE BOOKS   NEW YORK

Published in the United States by One World Books,
an imprint of The Random House Publishing Group,
a division of Random House, Inc., New York.

ONE WORLD is a registered trademark and the One World
colophon is a trademark of Random House, Inc.

Library of Congress Cataloging-in-Publication Data
Mills-Francis, Karen.
Stay in your lane : Judge Karen's guide to living your best life /
Karen Mills-Francis, in collaboration with Roy L. Brunson
and Veronica Mills-Raymond.
p. cm.
ISBN 978-0-345-52483-6
eBook ISBN 978-0-345-52484-3
1. Conduct of life.   2. Self-realization.   3. Mills-Francis, Karen.
I. Brunson, Roy L.   II. Mills-Raymond, Veronica.   III. Title.
BJ1581.2.M556 2010
170'.44—dc22   2010019685

Printed in the United States of America

www.oneworldbooks.net

2 4 6 8 9 7 5 3 1

FIRST EDITION

Book design by Carol Malcolm Russo

This book is dedicated to my parents,

Theodore and Andrea Mills,

and to my grandparents, Lee and Elvira McKinney

According to an old Hindu legend, there was a time when all men were gods, but they misused and abused their divinity. The chief god, Brahma, decided to take away man's divinity and hide it in a place where man would never again find it. Where to hide it became the big question.

When the minor gods were called together to consider this question, they said, "Let's bury man's divinity deep in the earth." But Brahma said, "No, that will not do, for man will dig deep down into the earth and find it." Then they said, "Well, then, we can take his divinity out to the deepest part of the ocean and submerge it there." But again Brahma replied, "No, not there, for man will soon learn to dive into the deepest waters and will search throughout the bottom of the ocean and will find it."

Then the minor gods said, "We will take it to the top of the highest mountain and hide it there." But again Brahma replied, "No, for man will eventually climb every high mountain on earth. He will be sure someday to find it and take it up again for himself." Then the minor gods simply gave up and concluded, "We do not know where to hide it, for it seems there is no place on land or in the sea that man will not eventually reach."

Then Brahma said, "I have an idea. We will hide man's divinity deep down inside of man himself, for he will never think to look for it there." Ever since then, the legend concludes, man has been going up and down the earth, climbing, digging, diving, exploring, searching for something that is already inside of himself.

Contents

Introduction

My judicial background inspires me to live my life inside the context of truth and justice. This, combined with many personal and life-altering experiences, qualifies me to speak the truth, the whole truth, and yes, sometimes the bitter truth. We all have a unique story, one that speaks of the trials and tribulations that make up the human condition, but at the end of the day, we are more alike in our similarities than we are different in our differences. This book represents some of the lessons learned from my own unique experiences, lessons that I hope you too can learn from.

Because I am a judge with my own television show, some people might think that I am removed from the realities of everyday life. While my audience may see me on TV, people have only a glimpse into who and what I am and strive to be. To some, I am a no-nonsense, polished, consummate professional. Let me assure you, though, there is plenty of "my stuff," which I continue to work on each and every day of my life. Although I have lived a full and remarkably wonderful life with few regrets, I have had my share of high points, low points, and downright heartache. These life experiences, good and bad, have made me who I am today.

I am the oldest of five children and Auntie Karen to ten nieces and nephews. Throughout the course of my life I have faced a gamut of difficult and conflicting challenges. I was raised in a one-bedroom apartment with seven people, declared a truant child at age eight by the state of Florida, and ended up applying for, and receiving, food stamps. As I got older, life did not necessarily become less of a challenge. I have had my lights and telephone disconnected, been placed in the backseat of a police car, had a car repossessed, been held at gunpoint in a drug raid, and have been witness to, and victim of, real domestic violence. My employment has included being everything from a restaurant dishwasher to a maid in other people's homes to working as a sales girl at JCPenney. But I have also sailed across the Hong Kong harbor, celebrated my birthday at an oceanfront estate on the Pacific coast of Mexico, planted a tree at the base of Mt. Kilimanjaro, and even been attacked by a baboon on an African safari.

In the courtroom, as well as in my personal life, I have drawn on my past experiences time and again to shape my decisions on the bench and to help keep me grounded. It's fitting that the slogan I used when running for judge was "Sensitive to All." I have walked in your shoes, and I have seen your darkest hour. Life may have gotten more financially comfortable for me over time, but as I witness the pain and suffering of adults and children who cross my path daily, I am moved to help guide them to being whole, as I have been so guided. And I continue to be guided because learning to live your best life is not a destination, it is a perpetual journey. I meet many people who are hurting and lost because they did not have the wisdom of elders to help lead them in their life journey. Through my own light and dark times, I have always had my mother, father, grandparents, and others who were and continue to be excellent role models. Such blessings are meant to be shared. Martin Luther King, Jr., said: "The ultimate measure of a man is not where he stands in moments of comfort and convenience, but where he stands at times of challenge and controversy." In these times of financial greed, shameless self-aggrandizement, and a disconnected, Internet-ruled world, I find myself believing that these are the times Dr. King spoke of: times of challenge and controversy.

At this very moment in my life I feel called upon to step up to the plate and share what I have learned along the way. I know for certain that numerous people are having trouble maintaining a job, paying mortgages, making relationships work, and raising their kids, let alone planning for the future. Every time I sit at the bench in my courtroom, I face people who feel as if they are sinking. Their lives have become full of drama. It may sound too simple to say that all this stems from people not staying in their lane, but I believe that's not far from the truth. Staying in your lane is not simply about minding your own business. Rather, it's about *focusing* on your business and improving your circumstances using common sense. When you focus on your business you don't have time to cross other people's boundaries, which is the root of most conflicts. Imagine if we all stayed true to our own course, focusing on what we need to get done: There would be fewer dramas, conflicts, and hurt feelings, and more purpose, direction, and powerful living.

In *Stay in Your Lane* what I have to say isn't always going to be pretty; sometimes staying in your lane means taking off the kid gloves and speaking the truth, even when it stings. I'm going to help you learn how to do that from a place of respect and love, and not with an intention to hurt. I'm not spouting some New Age fad, but a *commonsense approach to living* your best life by calling on those innate qualities buried within you. Each of us has a powerful compass that helps us figure out the right path to follow, helps us sift truth from lies. And sometimes that compass needs to be recalibrated. My whole purpose in writing *Stay in Your Lane* is to help you find your way back to *that voice within you* that knows more about how you should live your life than all the experts combined.

Yes, we live in a fast-paced world, and that can increase the challenge of operating from our own best instincts. However, that is no excuse to be ignorant, discourteous, or downright lacking in generosity of spirit and deeds. We must always continue to expect the best from ourselves and others. We must continue to break barriers and go outside our comfort zones, and we must seek truth above all else. That is what growth is all about.

Because I interact with "lost souls" all day long, and simultaneously work on figuring out who I want to be in this world, I have come to understand that life is like a road trip across a vast country. As you embark upon your trip you must first make sure that your vehicle has been serviced and is capable of making the trip. Then you must get a quality road map to study. This book offers you one to consider. You will note that there are several ways to get from point A to point B. The goal is not time oriented but rather quality oriented. The first and most important rule of the road is to do no harm. If you need to take a longer route to get to your final destination, that's okay, as long as you do unto others as you would have them do unto you. Enjoy the view and enjoy the ride! Life is an incredible journey—just respect the road and read the signs carefully, and you will arrive safely. And whether you drive your vehicle quickly or slowly, always remember to Stay in your lane!

I

WEAVING YOUR WAY OUT OF THE TRAFFIC JAM CALLED "THE PAST"

Take a Detour Down Memory Lane

When I first went into private practice as a criminal defense attorney, I was invited to a cocktail party thrown by the state bar association. Since childhood, I had known that I wanted to be a lawyer and now I was finally stepping into this ancient and noble profession. The event was going to be held at a swanky five-star hotel in South Miami, and I was eager for the chance to hobnob with my colleagues. Here was my opportunity to rub shoulders with the best in the field.

All week long I considered multiple outfits and the things I would say and the people I would say them to. And as I finally settled on the perfect pair of pumps, I suddenly got slammed with a strong mental image of my car. As I thought about driving my dented and faded ten-year-old car up to the valet line of that hotel with all the sparkling BMWs, Mercedes-Benzes, and Jaguars, I panicked. I decided right then and there that I could not go to the event.

Later as I lay in bed thinking about my decision, I wondered why I felt so ashamed. Was this really about my car? Or was it something deeper? I realized that the fear that gripped my heart had nothing to do with my car. It was the fear of being ridiculed. I was afraid that my poverty would show. In my mind the car put me in the category of the "have-nots."

It's funny how things that happened so long ago, things that you think are buried in the past, can affect your current outlook. But when I reflected on my childhood, I realized that there was one period of time in particular that was contributing to my dread of the cocktail party. You see, when I went to grade school, mothers dressed their daughters like baby dolls. The girls in my class would come to school in crinoline dresses with petticoats underneath and large silk bows in their hair. They dressed like Shirley Temple, right down to the candy curls. My parents had four other children and could not afford to dress me that way. They spent any extra money they had on buying books for me and my siblings. I stood out like a sore thumb among my classmates, who teased me for my shabby dresses and worn-out shoes. I felt like a Doberman in a room full of poodles. It got to the point where every morning before going to school I would throw a tantrum. I guess I always had a flair for drama! And now, twenty-five years later, here I was still crying and screaming and carrying that insecure "poor girl" around with me like a handbag into my adulthood.

It was a real dark night of emotions, and my soul felt so heavily burdened. As I relived the feelings of the past, I had a wake-up moment. I became mad at myself and began to shout out loud, "Didn't your parents make sure you had a good foundation so that you could have a career? Hadn't they sacrificed their own comfort so that you and your brothers and sisters could have a fair chance to rise above the circumstances of race and class? And didn't you fight and claw your way through college and law school, washing dishes in restaurants, borrowing from Peter to pay Paul, all to realize the dream of becoming a lawyer?" I realized that the long journey to my dream entitled me to pull up to the front door of that hotel right along with the Bentleys. Shoot, I was entitled to get up to that door on camel back if I had to. I was embarrassed by my selfishness and short-sightedness. There are people in this world who don't even have a car, I thought. I pass some of them at bus stops every day in all kinds of weather. They would probably give anything to be driving my ten-year-old car. My problems were nothing compared to what others must do simply to survive from one day to the next. And here I was, a thirty-year-old lawyer with a private practice, wearing grown-up clothes, still carrying the weight of that sniveling six-year-old around with me.

When I was six it was understandable that I would have

those feelings of not being good enough because I wasn't yet mentally and emotionally equipped to handle them and therefore didn't know any better. But as an adult who had overcome many obstacles and who had learned many lessons, with many more to come, I needed to make peace with the past in order to face the future. I made the decision that night to stop feeling inadequate and sorry for myself. I told myself, "No one who comes across your path has walked in your shoes. From now on, you are equal to anybody you meet for the duration of your lifetime." I had released six-year-old Karen.

Our life's journey is hard enough without the weight of all the baggage we carry with us from our past. As sure as my name is Judge Karen, life will test us and twist us in ways that are unimaginable. Just staying squarely on the road as we move toward our destination will at times be a challenge. We cannot move toward living our best life if our eyes are always looking in the rearview mirror.

It is amazing how we, as adults, are shaped and impacted by words, gestures, and actions that someone may have thrown our way when we were children, whether well-intentioned or not. Childhood hurt is real and can and will weigh us down if we never deal with it, like those taunts I received from my classmates. I urge you to get a shovel and dig up the past, shake it up, and kick it up, and when you're done, make peace with it and then let it go. You need to be looking ahead toward the dreams and goals I know you have. I invite you to think about the baggage that you are carrying and how it is affecting the quality of your journey. While I admit that it's not always easy to let go, I assure you that you'll get further ahead with a carry-on bag than you will with a steamer trunk. There is always a time and a place for the past, but the destination for you and me is on the road ahead.

As you begin this new journey, take time to assess what is in your rearview mirror. It will take a lot of hard work and introspection, but I promise you it will be worth it in the end. A good starting place to look for stuff you need to unload will usually be your childhood. Some of you have been through a lot of heavy stuff, maybe more than any child should bear witness to. And if that is true for your particular situation, then I strongly urge you to seek professional help and guidance as you navigate your way through some potential land mines. There is absolutely nothing wrong with talking to a professional about what is eating away at you. Mental and emotional stress is just as dangerous as any physical injury you might experience. In today's society, there is no stigma in seeing a psychologist or psychiatrist.

I have reached a verdict. Our total well-being matters in every aspect of our lives, and it is this court's order that you take care of all of "you," inside and out. You need to be looking ahead toward your dreams and goals. You can never have a second chance at a happy childhood. But there is always a chance for a happy adulthood. So make peace with the past and let's go!

▐━

"To live completely, wholly, every day as if it were a new loveliness, there must be dying to everything of yesterday, otherwise you live mechanically, and a mechanical mind can never know what love is or what freedom is."

—Jiddu Krishnamurti

Princess Problems

Once during a court recess I rushed back upstairs to my chambers on a purely personal mission. I was searching online retailers, looking for a gown to wear to an upcoming judicial ball. For two or three days, I had spent my recesses and lunch hour feverishly scouring department store online outlets for the perfect dress to wear to the annual event. I had gained a reputation for always strutting into that judicial ball in a stunning gown. But this year, I looked at hundreds of dresses, unable to settle upon something worth talking about. And I was getting flustered that I could not find the perfect, drop-dead gorgeous dress to wear. My secretary said, "Judge, why can't you wear the dress you wore three years ago? Nobody will remember." I said, "Shush your mouth!

How can I ruin my reputation by wearing the same dress twice to an event?" I actually was close to crying and getting depressed that I was down to the wire and might just have to repeat a gown I had worn before. But I had to put the search on hold until my next recess and hurriedly put on my robe to go back down to the courtroom. Seated back on the bench, I have to admit that I was a little distracted by my dress dilemma when the clerk called up my next case.

The woman who appeared at the podium had been before me several times, and she never forgot to bring her attitude with her. I was definitely not in the mood to deal with her that day. Her teenage daughter had been skipping school and getting into fights. When she went to discuss her daughter's case with the school officials, this short-tempered woman ended up grabbing a chair and throwing it through a window. She was arrested for destruction of school property and came before me on the charges. The first time she came to court, you could see how irritated she was. Arms crossed, sucking her teeth, exhaling heavily, and rolling her eyes! She looked like a bull seeing red. Because this was her first criminal offense, she was sent to an anger-management program. The program cost $175, but she said she could not pay for it. Based on the financial form she filed with the clerk's office, I agreed to waive the fee for the program. The prosecution agreed to dismiss her charges once she successfully completed the program in five to eight weeks. Real simple.

She just couldn't do it! She never seemed to be able to complete the sessions and kept being sent back to court for not showing up. I kept reenrolling her, and she kept ditching the sessions. Let me tell you, she was jumping up and down on my last nerve! I was beginning to lose my patience with her! By the third or fourth time she came back to court for noncompliance, I was at my wits' end. I told her that she had been given more than enough opportunities to close the case, and now I was prepared to find her in contempt of court. I was prepared to throw her in jail right there on the spot. So I appointed an attorney to represent her. He took her into the jury room, and I could hear her screaming at the top of her lungs. "I don't care what she does to me! I don't care about the program! I don't care about my children! I don't care if I go to jail! I—just—don't—care—anymore!" Then I heard loud wailing sounds coming from the jury room. When they came back into the courtroom half an hour later, the woman's eyes were bloodshot and her face swollen from tears. This big, tough woman who had nothing but attitude every time she came to court now looked so small and defeated.

Her lawyer spoke for her. She and her husband had moved to Miami from the West Coast after he lost his job in a bank. He convinced her to leave her job, her family, and her life to come to Miami with him and start over. Once they moved, the husband learned that there was a warrant out for his arrest stemming from something he had done while working at the bank. He promptly cleaned out what little money they had in their account and abandoned her, their son, and two daughters, leaving them to fend for themselves. They were evicted from their apartment and their belongings put out on the sidewalk. They had no money for a storage unit, so they lost most of what they had to thieves and the weather. She and the children slept inside of her car for weeks before the woman found a part-time job. She had no friends or family in the area and was doing her best to feed her children and keep them in school. She was hoping to save enough money to get them all back to the West Coast, but she lost the part-time job because she had to attend the anger-management sessions and come to court. The woman and her children were living in a motel room that cost $150 a week, and she was being evicted. The lawyer held up the eviction notice. The eviction was for that very day! The woman held her head down and cried the entire time the lawyer was speaking, and I could see how ashamed she was to have everybody in that courtroom hear how life had dealt her such a heavy blow. I also was struck by the burden she carried.

Despite the meanness I see in the world, I know for a fact that people are basically good. That day, several of the lawyers standing around in the courtroom reached into their pockets and started a collection to help this woman pay her rent. Some of the other defendants and onlookers chipped in money too that day. I believe that they raised more than $400, which they handed to her. And the prosecutor dismissed her case! The better angels of mankind reveal themselves at the darnedest of times, usually in moments when we need them the most. That woman needed heaven's mercy at that hour in a big way. Her salvation came right on time.

A little of my own salvation came that day too. Here I was obsessing and whining over not being able to find a new dress to wear to a $250-a-plate formal and thinking "poor, pitiful me." Actually (I have never told anyone this before) I ended up giving the woman money too. And I ended up choosing one of the many gowns in my closet to wear to the ball that year. This woman's life circumstances, and those of others I have met since, showed me that I was becoming shallow and superficial in some aspects of my own life. I was heading down a path that made me appear self-absorbed and fake. That is one of the good things about our journey. We can always turn off of any road we find ourselves traveling that is not leading us closer to greater awareness and personal growth. The road I was on at that time was paved with vanity. In discarding the belief that I had to be the belle of the ball, I was liberated! This new revelation allowed me to shift gears and redirect my focus to what I was toting around in my mind and wearing inside my heart.

What some of us consider necessities—beauty appointments, dry cleaning, dinner, and a movie—would be luxuries for others. When you realize this fact, some of what you call "problems" are just petty inconveniences. I have a good friend, Mike, whom I met a couple of years ago. Whenever I find myself whining to him, he says. "Hey, you know, that's not a real problem, that is only a princess problem." And then I feel like someone stuck a big pin in my balloon and brought me back down to earth. But on earth is where I always strive to be. It is firmer ground. Now, whenever I hear myself sounding melodramatic over something I can't do or have, I have learned to ask *myself,* "Karen, is this a real problem or a princess problem?"

Each of us has challenges that we deal with daily, and I cannot say to you that your problems are not more or less important than someone else's. We all look at things through our own personal lenses and from our own point of view. But I know for certain that *all* of us have princess problems! How many times have you said, "I don't have anything to wear to work today," when you have clothes that you just don't feel like wearing? Or you want a fancy car like your sister's when there is absolutely nothing wrong with the car you are driving? We can learn to immediately rank "problems" in degrees of importance. Ask yourself, is this thing that I am losing sleep over and complaining about something that will change or threaten my life? Ninety-nine percent of the time it isn't. You know when you are experiencing a princess problem because it arises from a sense of vanity and selfishness. It comes from a false sense of entitlement or from comparing ourselves to others whose lives we believe somehow dictate which direction our own should be going. Princess problems cause us to over-magnify the importance of events in our lives. We make them bigger than they really are in the grand scheme of things. I try to think of problems in relation to those of the majority of the world. Just the fact that you, dear reader, can sit down to a dinner every night and lay your head down in your own bed rather than under a bridge is a feat in itself. Let's strive to keep our problems in context. Life presents enough real challenges on its own without our having to throw in our own imaginary ones. The next time you think you're having a problem or you declare that something going on in your life is "just horrible" ask yourself, "Is this a real problem? Or am I having a princess problem today?"

———

"I cried because I had no shoes, until I met a man with no feet."
—PERSIAN PROVERB

If You Lie Down with Dogs You Will Get Fleas

I don't know how many times I have admonished juveniles (and some adults) who come into my courtroom that "You are the company you keep." There was a young man in particular, Robert, whom I met in court. He was a perfect example of how surrounding yourself with the wrong crowd can never lead to anything good. Robert was a good child, and I became his mentor during five critical years of his life. I knew he had a good heart. But when he became a teenager he started hanging out with ne'er-do-wells. His friends barely went to school, hung out late at night, and were definitely involved in drug activity. I would tell him, "Robert, if you lie down with dogs you will get fleas." He asked me what I meant, and I told him, "If you hang out with people who are doing nothing with their lives, then you are going to end up doing nothing with yours." He assured me that he knew his limits and how to balance his life. "I got this!" he told me. He was convinced that he was in control.

And then it happened. Robert ended up being arrested, along with four of his "dogs," for possession of stolen property. He was totally flea-infested by then. And a flea-infested dog is in danger of infesting other living beings he comes into contact with. His arrest made me question whether I could continue to allow him to come over to my house to hang out with my young nephews. There was no way I would jeopardize their safety by having someone around them who was a bad influence. But something about Robert told me he could still be saved. I agreed to go to bat for him in his court case if he promised to graduate high school and move away for a while. He agreed.

After high school, Robert went to live with a male relative of mine in North Carolina for a year. This relative is a no-nonsense type of guy who, I knew, would not let Robert get away with being irresponsible in his home. There Robert learned structure and responsibility. My relative had Robert volunteering every weekend to feed the homeless; he was enrolled in classes at a trade school during the day and worked at night. He was required to pay rent, and he had house and yard duties. During this time, Robert really became a man, in every sense of the word. When he came back home to Miami, he told me he had a chance to meet up with some of his former "dogs." He was shocked by the realization that their lives in the past year had been as stagnant as standing water. Nothing about their activities, conversation, or behavior had changed one bit. Same stuff, different day. "I understand now what you were saying about those people, Ms. Mills," he said. "How they are never going to do anything with their lives, and as long as I hung with them I wouldn't do anything with mine! They don't make plans, and their yesterday is no different from their today. I am planning for my tomorrows." What a man!

I'm happy to say that Robert has since graduated from college and plays football in Canada. He is no star player, a benchwarmer really, but he has a well-paying job and sponsors a program that mentors at-risk high school boys. He now steers clear of those dogs. That trip to North Carolina was a real flea dip; he was able to rid himself of the negativity and bad habits with which his friends of choice were infested.

This lesson doesn't apply just to children. Maybe you or someone you know needs a dusting of flea powder. Women who have negative friends who gossip or indulge in unhealthy living practices need to get up from around those dogs too. Remember, misery loves company, and you are the company you keep. Men with friends who drink all day or womanize may need a flea bath to rid themselves of *that* bad company. You will never become anybody if you surround yourself with a bunch of nobodies. It boils down to living *your* life with a sense of your *own* purpose.

—

"If you wallow in the mud with pigs, you will never be able to soar through the mountains with eagles."

–JUDGE KAREN

Where Is Your Moral Compass Leading You?

When I was a criminal defense attorney in 1991, I tried a case in front of a judge who, for purposes of this story, we'll call Judge Jesse. I knew him when he had been a prosecutor. Back then, he had been a friendly and agreeable person who was well liked in the courthouse and in the community. Then he ran for circuit court judge in Miami. His victory at the age of thirty-three made him among the first black men to be elected to the circuit bench. With his new $90,000-a-year salary, he and his wife promptly moved into a mansion. As a new judge, he caught a case of what we in the legal profession call "robe fever," meaning that he let his power to determine people's fate go to his head. He grew mean and cocky and developed a reputation for keeping lawyers and litigants in court for eighteen-hour days. Once, while on the bench, he said he was a king! He often went on screaming tirades in his courtroom and once threw two people in jail because they didn't want to accept his plea offer to their cases. The appellate court promptly ordered their release the same night.

During the trial I had before him, his trial order was that we would start each day at ten a.m. and work until two o'clock in the morning, reconvening each day again, eight hours later, at ten a.m. It seemed strange to me that he would take breaks of only five minutes between hours and hours of testimony and that many of the breaks happened at the most inopportune times during trial: in the middle of a cross-examination, near the end of arguments on a motion, and he even took one smack in the middle of his reading of the jury instructions. I noticed a young woman sitting quietly in the back of the courtroom whom I recognized as a clerk who worked in the courtroom of another judge. She was there when we took recess each night, and I couldn't imagine why she was there since she was not involved in either the prosecution or defense case for this trial.

At the end of the testimony, as we were about to begin closing arguments, the judge told us he was limiting our arguments to eight minutes. This was unheard-of! I argued to him that there had been three days of testimony and a lot of evidence introduced, and that the defense needed at least thirty minutes to give the closing argument to the jury. He screamed that his words were final, he was the judge, and he set the rules, and if we did not want to abide by them we would face contempt charges and jail! So we limited our argument to the time allowed, asking for more time at the end of those paltry eight minutes. The judge denied the request and proceeded to read the final jury instructions. The defendant was found guilty, and the defense promptly filed an appeal. The conviction would later be reversed on appeal based on the time limitation for closing arguments ordered by the judge.

A few weeks after the trial, I had just returned to my office from court when I noticed the office staff hovering around the television inside the break room. The local programming had been interrupted for breaking news. There was Judge Jesse on the television screen in handcuffs being hauled off on federal charges for accepting thousands of dollars in bribes to fix criminal cases. He was among five judges indicted in what is still the largest judicial corruption sting in U.S. history. And the lady who brought him down to his knees was the woman who had sat in the back of the courtroom throughout the trial. She was his lover.

Within months Judge Jesse was suspended from the bench and permanently disbarred from practicing law. He is currently serving a twenty-year prison sentence for theft of public funds. He disappointed a lot of people. Many blacks and Hispanics in Miami were overjoyed to have elected a man of color to the bench. They believed his campaign speeches when he promised he would be a fair and impartial jurist of whom they could all be proud. They believed him when he said he would use his judicial office to develop programs to help give direction to youth. Not only did he let power go to his head, but he also abused the office that he swore to uphold and honor. His life veered out of control because he had no positive guiding principles orchestrating his choices. No code or compass based on integrity informed his journey. We all need this moral compass to give us directions for the road ahead. It sets the ground rules that keep us on track. It points us in the right direction and discourages us from taking wrong turns. It is the light that we can depend on to always illuminate the right course of action.

Some of you might defend your lack of moral code by saying, "There was no sense of honor or decency in my home growing up." Or you see instances of depravity in national sports figures, the media, and politicians, and question why any of the rest of us are expected to live an honorable and ethical life. I have a better question. If others are living amoral or dishonorable lives, what does that have to do with the road *you* are traveling on? You were born alone and you will die alone. For me, this fact is enough confirmation that it is up to me to make sure I stay in *my* lane and find *my* own direction. In the end, it will only be between my God and me.

If you have been given a brain to think with and a heart to love with, then you have all the tools you need to learn and incorporate positive guiding principles into your own life. Just the fact that you want to do so means it's already somewhere inside of you, needing some help to get out. You can look for role models at work, in your church, or among your family and friends. There is someone somewhere in your sphere whom you have the utmost respect for because of the inspiring way they are conducting their lives. Talk to them, learn from them. You can also start reading books to raise your awareness, books written by and about men and women who lived uplifting and upstanding lives. History is full of such people: Mother Teresa, Maya Angelou, Mahatma Gandhi, Nelson Mandela, Eleanor Roosevelt, and Harriet Tubman are just a few. Notice that this small list includes people of different races and nationalities. There are thousands of others.

It has been said that "the unexamined life is not worth living." I am inviting you to examine your life right now. Do you have a moral code of conduct that governs your every turn? What is that code? And if you don't have one, then now is the time to find it. Are you ready?

⊢

"The time is always right to do what is right."
—MARTIN LUTHER KING, JR.

The Greatest Love of All

One of my favorite songs of all time is "The Greatest Love of All" from the movie *The Greatest*. The lyrics were written by a young mother, Linda Creed, who was struggling with breast cancer. The meaning of the song has always resonated with me. "Learning to love yourself is the greatest love of all."

As a young girl I always dreamed of having a better life. Maybe that came from being raised in a two-parent household where I was encouraged, loved, and nurtured. The outlook for my four siblings and me to succeed in life was not just a hope, but an expectation established by my parents when we were young children. As a result of my family's love and belief in me, I learned to love myself at a very young age. I wish every young girl could experience that type of love because it grounds you. Unfortunately, this is not always the case. The tragic lives of young girls play out every day in our cities and neighborhoods, often without voice or eyes to record their sorrow and despair. The following story may be very painful to read, but I believe it's important that it be told. It has inspired me and continues to motivate me to help women to struggle beyond their past hurts and disappointments and learn to not only survive, but thrive by building futures full of hope and possibilities.

In December 2007, while still on the bench in Miami, I participated in a Christmas toy drive to collect gifts for children living with their mothers in domestic violence shelters. The shelters were operated by the SafeSpace Foundation, which provides food, shelter, counseling, and job referral services for women fleeing an abusive household. Through the toy drive, I met the president of the foundation, who invited me to come to the shelter to meet with and talk to some of the women residents. I did not know what to expect. What I found were normal women who were living in fear. Fear of retaliation from a boyfriend or spouse, fear of not being able to provide for their children, and fear of the future. Some women I talked with sounded confident that by coming into the shelter, they had turned a corner on a past full of beatings and fights. I talked to others who were seriously thinking about leaving the shelter to return to their abusive situation because they missed the offender or needed him for financial support. There were also women in the shelter who were still in denial about the abuse, blaming themselves for someone else's violent temper.

As I was milling around waiting for the evening's program to start, I met an incredible woman named Norvell Holyfield. She came to the shelter that day because she wanted to share her journey with the women in transition. I believe hers is a journey in which we can all find inspiration. It is with her permission that I tell you her story.

In May 1991, Norvell met Christopher, whom she found to be an incredibly passionate and romantic man, and within a few months she had fallen in love. In October of that year, Norvell and Christopher went on a day trip to Key West to attend a festival with a group of coworkers. On the bus ride back home that evening, Christopher was very drunk and started calling Norvell names. Upset and embarrassed, Norvell moved away from him and sat in a different seat. Christopher began roaming up and down the bus calling for her and getting more and more belligerent when he couldn't find her. Everyone kept telling him that Norvell was right in front of him, but he was so drunk he couldn't recognize her. When he did locate her, he said, "You trying to embarrass me in front of these people!" When the bus arrived back in Miami, Norvell asked a man on the bus to drop her at home, but unknown to her, he had been directed by Christopher to drop her off at Christopher's house instead.

It was three a.m., so Norvell decided to go inside. Christopher was in his forties and lived at home with his mother. Once Christopher and Norvell were in his room, he began beating her. He grabbed her by the hands and broke her finger and beat her in the face until she was bloodied and swollen. After what seemed like an eternity of Norvell's screams and cries, his mother ran into the room yelling, "Don't fight her, baby." She asked him why he was beating Norvell, and he said, "Mama, she won't lay with me." His mother said, "She'll lay with you, baby." She wiped the blood off Norvell's face, undressed her, and laid her on the bed. Christopher got in bed next to her and promptly fell into a drunken slumber. Then his mother left the room. The next morning Norvell crept out of Christopher's room, hoping to escape quietly as he slept off the liquor. His mother was in the kitchen drinking coffee. She asked Norvell where she was going, and Norvell said, "I need to get to the doctor. I think my finger is broken and I can barely open my eyes. " Christopher's mother calmly looked up and told Norvell, "If you go to the hospital, Christopher will get in trouble. Just go lie down. I'll take care of you." For the next week, Christopher and his mother kept Norvell in the apartment. There were bars on all of the windows and locks on all the doors. Norvell was a captive. Eventually, Christopher drove her to the doctor and then right back to his house. He noticed the change in Norvell after his brutal attack on her. He said, "You don't laugh at my jokes anymore or make love to me the same. But it's okay. Because you disrespected me, I had to do that." This was the very first time he hit her. But she believed him when he said it was the last. So she stayed.

It was shortly after the beating that Norvell learned of Christopher's dependence on drugs and alcohol. In July 1992, she convinced him to go to an Alcoholics Anonymous meeting and went with him. During the meeting, Norvell went to the lobby to get a cup of coffee. When she returned, Christopher told Norvell that she couldn't drink it because he couldn't consume any type of caffeine. This is when she had what Oprah calls "an 'aha' moment." Norvell said to herself, "If he isn't even in control of himself enough for me to be able to drink a cup of coffee, then I don't need to be with him." That is when she made the decision to try to break away from Christopher for good. As a gift, she gave him an expensive pair of sneakers that he'd really wanted. Her mother always said, "Give a man a pair of shoes if you want him to leave you." Norvell thought to herself, "Now he can walk away in style!" But he didn't leave. He just continued to walk all over her. Eventually, however, she gathered the courage to leave him.

In September 1992, Norvell was laid off from her job and Christopher started calling her for some reason. He called her all day and left threatening messages: "Pick up the phone, bitch! If you don't answer this f—king phone, you'll see what happens!" Worried for her safety, a female friend came to Norvell's apartment to spend the night with her. Christopher continued to make harassing calls and leave obscene messages on her answering machine. Norvell thought that the harassing and threatening phone calls were not evidence enough to get the police involved so she never dialed 911. She was right. His actions were not a crime at the time they took place, although today his actions would amount to criminal stalking.

The next morning as her friend was getting ready to leave for work, Norvell heard a light tap at the door. She looked out through the peephole and didn't see anyone. She called security to find out if anyone had come into the building asking for her. The guard said no but offered to come check her hallway for intruders. Norvell lived on the eighth floor, in the very last apartment in her hallway, across from the fire exit. When security checked outside her door, they found no one. Norvell called Christopher's mother and told her about his harassment and asked where he was. His mother replied, "He ain't worried about you, he is in his bed. I told him there are more women in the world than you, Norvell." Norvell decided that his mother was probably right. Maybe the light tap she had heard at the door was just the result of her jumpy nerves. Norvell turned to her friend and said, "Well, if you're not scared to walk out the door, I'm not scared to open it." And with that, Norvell pulled the door open.

Christopher came rushing out of the fire exit door and into the apartment. He had a large butcher knife and began stabbing Norvell as her friend screamed. He stabbed her in her face, head, and collarbone and only stopped when the knife got lodged in her collarbone. He turned to her friend and said, "Get out because I'm gonna kill this bitch." As he led the friend out the door, Norvell went to her glass patio doors and looked out to her balcony. She looked down, then back at Christopher, who was heading toward her fast.

As she reached to open the sliding door, he quickly came up from behind, grabbed her by the shoulder, and asked her where she thought she was going. He pulled her back into the apartment and sat her down on the couch, then sat next to her in silence. She started thinking of what she could say to convince this man to spare her life. She lied: "I still love you. I won't tell the police you hurt me. Please, please let me live." He kept repeating, "You made me do this, you wouldn't talk to me." Then he picked up the phone to call his mother and said, "Momma, I just stabbed Norvell, it's over." Norvell asked him for the phone and tried to convince his mother to talk to her son and dissuade him from harming her further. His mother said there was nothing she could do and hung up the phone. His mother never called the police.

Downstairs in the parking lot, Norvell's friend was in so much shock that she couldn't speak. She couldn't tell the security guard what happened or ask him to call the police. When she came to her senses, she began screaming the name of Norvell's neighbor, who lived in the complex. "Miiiiiiiiiike!" He had just left for work and had driven three blocks when he heard his name. What a miracle! Mike whipped his car around. Once he arrived, the friend told him, "He's killing Norvell!" Mike grabbed the Club that he used to lock his car's steering wheel and ran upstairs with the building's maintenance man. Mike rapped on the door, and when Christopher cracked the door to answer, Norvell sprang up behind him and reached her hand out through the doorway. Mike grabbed her arm and pulled her through the door. As her rescuers circled around her, Christopher rushed past them, left through the fire exit door, and ran down the stairs. He was trapped because the police were now there. When he saw the officers, Christopher walked up and surrendered himself, saying, "Call my mother so I can start life over." As police handcuffed Christopher, paramedics were placing Norvell in an ambulance on a gurney. Christopher yelled out to her, "I still love you, baby!"

In the hospital, Norvell received a three-way call from Christopher in jail and his mother at home. They both tried to convince Norvell to visit him in jail, make plans to marry him, and leave the incidents in the past. Hoping she wouldn't testify against Christopher, his mother said, "You have to lie for him if you love him." Hearing Christopher's voice sent Norvell into the corner of the room, shaking with terror. His mother repeatedly called Norvell and tried to bribe her not to testify by offering her gifts and trips, and she even offered to throw Norvell a big wedding. Once Norvell met with the prosecutor assigned to the case she found out that Christopher had seriously assaulted eight other women in the past. His mother had convinced them all to drop the charges! His mother had spent her life in Christopher's shadow, cleaning up the carnage left behind by his psychotic behavior and violent temper. When he was a teenager, Christopher had savagely beaten a neighbor's pet to death, and his mother had paid off the owner.

Unlike the other women, Norvell did not waver. Christopher was sentenced to eight years in prison for the attack. But Norvell could not move on. She believed that she still loved the man who had tried to kill her, an admission that she couldn't reveal to anyone. At the same time, she couldn't sleep at night because she was so afraid he would break out of jail and come harm her. She began to search deeper within herself for why she could accept violence in the place of real love.

When Norvell was five years old, her mother had gone to search for work up north and had left her with a relative she trusted to take care of her. At age five, Norvell was raped by a nineteen-year-old cousin. The relative sent her back to live with her newly married mother. Norvell's stepfather assaulted her too, saying that his marriage to her mother gave him rights to Norvell. She figured that love only came in the form of abuse. And so abuse led to her promiscuity and abusive relationships.

She began to see that she was no different than the victims of post-traumatic stress disorder. She learned that prolonged abuse is a shock to the system that you can't just stitch up or cover with a bandage. It takes more work to get to the root of the issue. Norvell saw that she had never taken the time to heal from the past and decided to start being a caretaker to herself. She said, "Women are so used to being caretakers that we forget to care for ourselves, leading to many mini-meltdowns, but we keep on going."

Norvell started allowing herself to heal, and she looked inside for answers as opposed to outside. She realized that she really did not love the person staring back at her in the mirror. She wore revealing clothes and heavy makeup to make the person in the mirror, the person she hated and treated with disdain, appear attractive. Her entire life had attracted a revolving door of abusive men. She realized that she had met a "Christopher" in every new city she had ever settled down in. Her ex-husband, boyfriends in Chicago, Pittsburgh, Miami, etc., had all beaten her. Christopher himself had told her that he watched her before he first approached her. He said he saw her walking with her head down and looking lonely and he knew exactly what he needed to do in order to get her. He was like a predator, stalking and waiting for the right time to pounce on just the right prey.

She began to focus her full attention on herself. She realized that being in these dramatic and abusive relationships kept the attention on the relationship or the abusive man, and never on her. She had a hand in what was happening to her life. She began exercising and eating better, and she threw away the revealing clothes and the heavy makeup. Norvell enrolled in college and, at age fifty, earned her associate's degree in business. She got a job working at a college and bought herself a new house and new car.

Norvell admits that she is still a work in progress, and she has dated new men, some good, some not so good. But she is operating from self-love, and that has been her greatest protection against bad relationships. When she feels herself going backward in thoughts and feelings, she shifts into a self-preservation mode by taking time out to read, write poetry, listen to music, meditate, and pray, which helps her regain strength and resolve. She says she makes certain that her life is always moving forward, and the road is getting better and brighter every day.

The words "I love you" are everywhere. They are printed on cards, coffee cups, calendars, and balloons. They are etched into sidewalks, trees, and bathroom stalls. And they constantly come from the lips of man- and womankind. If there were as much love as songs and poems profess, there would not be so much misery in life. It seems so easy for us to profess unconditional love for others. But the reality is, we cannot turn our hearts over to another until we have first claimed our undying love for ourselves. If we let someone whom we profess to love treat us like doormats, then we are not loving ourselves. I had to learn this the hard way too. I had to leave an abusive relationship of my own to realize that I had more "love" for my partner than I had for me. It's still not something I am comfortable talking about. But I can tell you from my own experience that your relationships will not become healthier and your path ahead will not become clearer until you put yourself first in your own heart. Take a look in the mirror. Gaze deeply into your own eyes and say "I love you." The first person you need to hear those words from is staring right back at you. If he or she is not saying it, then no matter how much you hear it from someone or somewhere else, the words are meaningless and you will be stalled on the side of the road. Start every day by saying " I love you" to yourself, and over time this habit will work miracles. You will start to treat yourself better and to expect better treatment from the people in your life. Just watch, your engine will start revving up. *You* will create the fuel you need for your journey. Before you know it, you will be back on your way. Just never stop looking out for yourself and treating yourself the way you expect to be treated by others. Always make your best "you" your number-one focus and everything else will start falling into place.

—

"In the end, the only thing you really own is your story. If you don't write it for yourself then someone else is going to write it for you."

—NORVELL HOLYFIELD

Bring Shame Back

One summer while in college in Maine, I stayed on campus because I could not afford to buy a ticket home. This was one of the poorest periods in my life. I have suffered financial strife before and since, but this time was different because I was alone and hundreds of miles away from my family. Brunswick, Maine, with a population of 12,000 when I lived there, is not a hotbed of gainful employment, especially for unskilled college students. The college allowed me to live on campus for no cost, but I had no money for the basic necessities, and my scholarship did not cover summer expenses. I applied for jobs at every business in town. I landed a three-week gig babysitting for a professor and his wife when their regular babysitter went on vacation. After that job there was nothing. I just could not find a company hiring in town. I started to get desperate, and desperate people do desperate things. At the height of my desperation, I walked into the local food stamp office and applied for food stamps. Someone told me that Congress had extended this program to college students. I thought that if I could at least buy groceries, then I could make it until the fall when school and my financial aid would start again. I felt uncomfortable sitting there in the waiting room waiting for my name to be called. As I was interviewed by a caseworker, I felt humiliated as she interviewed me about my financial status. Neither my parents nor their parents had ever applied for public assistance. But not only did I qualify for food stamps, they were given to me on an expedited basis. The first thing I did as soon as I got those food stamps was run down to the local grocery store to stock my refrigerator. I was so happy that day to be shopping for food again without worrying about having to skimp on the essentials or not having enough money at checkout. "God is good," I thought to myself. But my happiness rapidly faded once I had to deal with the cashier. That's when everything hit the fan.

As a line of other shoppers formed behind me, the clerk began ringing up my cart full of groceries. She announced the total and thrust her palm out for my money. When I handed the clerk the stamps, she looked at me with surprise and said in a voice that carried across the aisles and over to the other shoppers: "Why didn't you tell me that you were going to be using food stamps? You got stuff here you're not allowed to have. Didn't they tell you that at the food stamp office?" Irritated, she and the bag boy started tossing items out of my shopping bags to place back on the shelves. The line behind me had grown by several people by this time, and the rearranging of my grocery bags was causing a big delay. I felt my face growing very hot and prickly from the embarrassment, and I felt that all eyes were on me, whether it was true or in my imagination.

I felt ashamed. When I got back to my room, I called home collect, and my dad answered. I was crying as I told him how humiliated I had felt in the store. He knocked me off my feet with his response: "You *should* be feeling real ashamed of yourself. We never took food stamps or welfare and there are seven of us. There's only one of you. You are following your dream. It's up to you to make it happen without having to lift up your skirt or hold down your head." As ashamed as I had felt in that grocery store, the shame I felt from my father made me feel less than one inch tall. I felt not only that I had let him down, but that maybe I had taken an easy route without exhausting other alternatives. I vowed that I would *never* apply for or use food stamps again, there was just no way. I tossed the remainder into the trash and decided that I had to try harder to find other ways to survive. Then an idea came to me. I started going around to campus buildings and fraternity houses with a large plastic bag and collecting bottles and cans to redeem at the grocer's for cash. I had no shame showing up with cans and bottles once or twice a week to get money to buy what I wanted to buy, not from a selection that some-one else dictated. Eventually, I landed a job as a waitress in an ice cream restaurant and saved enough money to go home before school started in the fall.

I am not downing the food stamp program nor people who need it. There are many families suffering in these hard times of job losses and corporate downsizing who need the help that food stamps and welfare provide. Everybody needs a helping hand at some point in their lives. But I write here in this book about our individual and personal journeys. I am on this journey too. Staying in my lane means, among other things, always striving to be self-reliant, and thereby being my own person and not having someone dictate what I can or cannot have. It was the shame I felt from my father that brought this fact rushing back home to me. There is value in shame. Had I not felt the shame, I would not have tried harder to find ways to be self-reliant and independent.

Pop culture today convinces us to blame everything on something else. We are overweight, undereducated, fearful, insecure, in debt, or lonely because of our mothers, our childhood, our teachers, our race, our environment. Keeping our eyes on the outside somehow absolves us of the responsibility for ourselves. Nowadays we aren't supposed to make folks feel ashamed. It hurts their feelings. Their self-esteem. When I was a child, I used to have temper tantrums at home and they continued up until the time I went to first grade. I was a bit of a drama queen, and I learned early that these tantrums often got me attention and the things I wanted. I definitely was used to getting my way at home. That all ended my first day of grade school. Day one, I threw a hissy fit because I didn't like the seat I was assigned. Instead of giving in and letting me sit where I wanted, the teacher promptly sent me to sit in the corner for what felt like an eternity. I could hear the snickering of the other students behind my back. Hot tears rolled down my face. And that was my very last temper tantrum. Our teacher was an old-fashioned educator who walked around with a ruler in her hand, occasionally smacking a knuckle or two as she marched up and down the aisles of chairs. If you started "smelling yourself" and acting up, then she would send you to sit in a corner with your back to the rest of the classroom. And if you were *really* cuttin' up, like cursing or talking back, you got spanked in front of your classmates. The lesson we learned was that if you misbehaved, you would suffer dire and humiliating consequences for your behavior. The public beating, for us kids, was something on par with the seriousness of the death penalty. And it created such mortification that you tried to do everything in your power to stay out of trouble because of the fear of ridicule from your peers. To me, this method of raising children taught personal accountability and encouraged maturity. That's all outlawed now. Now, you can go to jail for doling out that type of discipline.

There was another teacher I remember from eighth grade who taught charm classes. Yeah, we had charm classes when I was a young girl. She would talk to us about the way we dressed ourselves. She always said: "Modesty is the best policy. Leave something to the imagination. A lady has sex appeal more for what she isn't revealing than what she has revealed." If she thought that one of us was dressed too provocatively, she would say "No self-respecting woman would carry herself that way. You ought to be ashamed of yourself." Shame kept boys from wearing their pants without belts and skipping school and mistreating girls. Shame kept girls from cursing and fighting. Shame and public humiliation were deterrents to sleeping around and having babies in high school. Today we are bombarded with so many, mostly negative, images of womanhood. It's popular to see "bad girls" and "wild girls" cursing and fighting on television and sleeping around. To me this behavior paints a picture of womanhood that is vulgar and, well, unladylike. The *New American Dictionary* defines a lady as a well-mannered and considerate woman with high standards of proper behavior. I think a lady is also independent in thought and action. I ask you to rise above any negative images the media is providing you on what it means to be a woman today. Living your best life means living your life honorably and respectfully, and, as my father said, without having to lift your dress up, or to hold your head down.

———

"There are so many examples of bad choices and scandalous behavior in the news today. It seems that society has misplaced its sense of decency and, as a result, has lost touch with the value of shame. A lack of shame is at the heart of much of the poor behavior we see around us in our personal lives and documented in the news."
–JOHN H. SKLARE

You Can Learn from the Past

I was an attorney in Miami for thirteen years before I became a judge. As a criminal defense lawyer, I represented defendants involved in some of the most treacherous activities you could imagine: rapists, robbers, murderers, you name it. I represented them all. But no matter the offense, if I agreed to accept a case, I represented that client like a bulldog. I can recall many sleepless nights preparing for a trial that would determine the direction a man's life would take. But the truth is, it became very frustrating over time. I would fight tooth and nail to secure a client's freedom, only to have him rearrested and taken back to jail, having made the same stupid choices time and again. Albert Einstein defined insanity as "doing the same thing over and over again and expecting a different result." If that is the definition, then I represented my fair share of lunatics! Some people learn from the mistakes of other people while others gain wisdom only through their own trials and errors. But there are those who learn to shift gears only when they are forced to face the gravest of life's truths. I want to tell you about fundamental lessons learned through a client I represented whom I'll call Gregory.

I liked Gregory. He was an extremely intelligent and well-spoken man. I thought that he really could have been an important and positive force in this world if he had grown up in a different environment. He was funny and sensitive, but he was *always* getting into trouble. He was a junior member of a very dangerous drug gang. I represented him on a case of possession of a firearm by a convicted felon. One day, as we were leaving a court hearing, we stood in front of the courthouse talking about his case. Out of nowhere, a man ran up from behind him and sucker punched Gregory in the face, knocking him down to the ground. He then kicked him a couple of times in the stomach and calmly walked away. I was speechless. Although the courthouse was crawling with police and security, no one came to our rescue. I asked Gregory afterward about the man. He brushed it off and told me he didn't know who the guy was.

Over the course of the next year, Gregory picked up more criminal charges, causing the court to revoke his original bond so he was taken to the county jail to await trial. While he was awaiting trial, the U.S. Attorney's Office lodged federal gun charges against Gregory based on the facts in the state's case. He was then transferred to a federal holding facility. Now we would have to shift gears, because he was facing a life sentence in federal court for the crime. In preparation for trial on his gun charge, I went to visit him in the federal jail in downtown Miami. I hated to see him there because I knew that this was now more serious than even he realized. Federal court is trial by ambush. The defense is not entitled to nearly as much discovery (evidence against the accused that the prosecution intends to use at trial) as we would get in state court. We sat at a table in the attorney interview room. I was busy looking through my files and telling Gregory that this trial was going to be an uphill battle. When I looked up at him over my glasses, he was staring into space. I asked him what was he thinking about. He never seemed very introspective, especially not when he met with me. With me, and probably most of his world, he was the tough street kid with tattoos and a mouth full of gold teeth.

After a long silence, he said, "You know, Miss Mills, I was a good student in elementary school. Can you believe that? I made all As and Bs and I loved getting up in the morning to go to school. I was always on time and had perfect attendance. I did my homework and in class I helped my teachers by cleaning the blackboard. I never got into trouble." I just listened to him without interrupting, because it seemed he was getting something off his chest. "I remember when I was in fourth grade, our entire class was preparing to put on a presentation of poetry in the school auditorium. Everybody had to learn the words to a poem and say it from heart on the stage. I was so excited that I would have a chance to say my poem in front of the entire school! The teacher said that we all had to wear a white button-down short-sleeve shirt; that we would not be allowed to be a part of the program if we did not wear the white shirt. She sent me home with a letter to my momma telling her that. Every day when I got home from school, I practiced saying my poem in the mirror. And I bugged my momma about the white shirt.

"The day before the program, when I got home from school, I asked my momma again about the white shirt. She was getting dressed to leave the apartment. I knew she had gotten her check. We lived right outside of downtown, and she said she was walking down to Woolworth to buy that shirt. Finally! I remember being so happy when I went to bed that night. Well, when I woke up for school the next morning, my momma was asleep on the floor in the living room and empty beer bottles and matchbooks were on the table. Then I saw the needles. She was passed out. Once again, momma had spent all her money on her heroin habit. No money left for my shirt. I had begged her for weeks about the shirt. Didn't she see how important it was to me, Miss Mills? I only asked for a shirt! I cried all the way to school that morning. I didn't get to say my poem. It was all over for me after that. From then on, I decided that I was going to have to find a way to take care of Gregory. If you depend on other people, you get disappointed. I dropped out of school at the end of that year. And you know the rest of the story."

Gregory's story always makes me sad. Even now, I think about what he could have become if things had only been different. Well, we won the federal trial. It was big news in Gregory's camp that he had beaten the federal rap. It was during the Christmas holiday season. Gregory called me from a pay phone to thank me again for the trial and to tell me that he had more good news in his life. He was going to be a father. He said "I don't want my son to have to grow up like I did." I told him that maybe God was giving him another chance to live right. He said he would be coming by my office before the holiday, that he had something to give me. We hung up. The next day I got a call that Gregory had been killed in a drive-by shooting. They said he was shot walking away from the pay phone after he hung up with me. He was twenty-two years old.

In 2008, I was visiting a community center in downtown Miami and autographing photos for fans of my show. A woman came up to me with a big smile on her face. She said she was the mother of a former client of mine. It was Gregory's mother! In the midst of all these people, his story from nearly a decade earlier came rushing back to me like a speeding train. She said that she was raising his son! "I made a lot of mistakes in my life with Gregory," she confessed. "I can't take back who and what I was back then. I know I wasn't a good mother to him. Then he left me with this child. The child's mother couldn't raise him. I believe God is giving me another chance. I am a nursing assistant now and work at a hospital. I moved to a better neighborhood. Gregory, Jr. is an A student, nine years old, and very active in school and sports." The news brought a smile to my face.

I am gratified every time someone learns from the hard lessons of their past. Gregory's mother summed it up best when she said that while it's too late for him, it's not too late for his son. I am not here to judge her past actions. I can only say that at the time she was going through whatever she was going through she did the best she was mentally and emotionally capable of doing. That does not absolve her from failing Gregory and driving both of their lives off the road. I am sure she is haunted by that every day of her life. But credit does go to her strength, resilience, and love for Gregory's memory and to her attempt to right her wrong.

If I've said it once, I've said it a thousand times: you can always redirect your path! The road to living your best life is not one etched in stone nor one paved with gold. Yours is a personal journey. As with all journeys, you may get lost on lonely roads or break down on dead-end streets. Sometimes you may even run out of gas. But as long as you have the will and passion to move onward, you have the means to get yourself going forward again. And so I say to you, dear reader, that no matter what you've been through and no matter how many mistakes you may have made along the way, you too can learn from your past and create a life that you want for yourself and the ones you love. Because there is always a tomorrow, there is always the possibility to get back large and in charge on your road of life. As always, it's your choice!

———

"Sometimes you find your destiny on the road you took to avoid it."

–Louis Salinger

II

FAMILY AND FRIENDS: DO YOU NEED TO ELIMINATE ANY EXCESS BAGGAGE?

The Complaint Department Is Closed for Renovations

I once had a neighbor named Joan who lived several houses down from me. She had been the first person to welcome me to the neighborhood. She had a beautiful garden, and we quickly developed a friendship. I loved being in her yard and learning about gardening from her. We ended up at each others' houses at least two or three times a week. She was extremely creative: She attracted hummingbirds to her backyard and created a sanctuary for them; she built all the furniture in her house and even had a koi pond at the front entrance. It was during this period of my life that I started having headaches and feeling down almost daily. My doctor said he could not find a reason for my symptoms. One day, when I was lying in my bed suffering through yet another headache, my young niece who was staying with me at the time said, "Auntie, you always have a headache when you've been around Miss Joan." Out of the mouths of babes! I started to think. Was it the hummingbirds? The fish? Something in her house? Then it came to me in a flash. It was Joan herself!

I thought back to our conversations. No matter how lightly they started, they always ended up in darkness. She would talk for hours about her alcoholic and abusive parents, her no-account ex-husband, and her substance-abusing best friend who had been dating a married man for thirty-five years. Joan rarely left her house except to run errands and visit me. She had few friends or visitors. And even though she was very smart and creative, her conversation always turned to the many ways life had disappointed her. I began to see that these interactions were draining me of my positive energy and causing me headaches. I decided to slowly wean myself away from her for her own good and my self-preservation.

In one of my last conversations with Joan, I told her that I thought she had made a decision to live like a hermit in order to avoid pain and disappointment, which are part of living. Later I sent her a card that had a quote that I have never forgotten: "Ships in the harbor are safe. But that's not what ships are built for." She seemed to understand that she had stopped living and was only existing, but she continued to throw pity parties nevertheless. It felt more comfortable to blame the people who had disappointed her in the past because it required less effort than taking full charge of her future. Eventually, we stopped communicating altogether. And I swear, my headaches and depression stopped altogether too! A few months later, I ran into one of my neighbors at the supermarket. He told me that Joan was finally pursuing a dream of hers. She had her master's degree in art appreciation, and she decided to accept a job as curator for a prominent museum. I was happy to hear her good news. See what happens when you stop being the crutch for an able-bodied person? They eventually learn to walk or to fall on their own. Either way, it's their journey. We cannot always shield people from their lessons.

Iyanla Vanzant wrote, "There are people sitting in the front row of your life who should be sitting in the balcony." After I read that I thought about the people sitting in the front row of my life. I took an evaluation of the people I was surrounded by, and I realized that because I am a good listener, many people came to me with their troubles. I am a problem solver by nature, but there were certain people who needed more than just my help. I had a couple of friends who seemed to have a rain cloud over their heads. It felt like there was never anything positive coming from them. There was unhappiness and negativity in every story they told. These people were draining my energy. I decided I needed to send them to the balcony. When friends like that come around, tell them, "I did not R.S.V.P for a pity party." Pity is no good for the person who's pitiful or for you as the person doling out the pity pennies. Sometimes you have to step back and even let them stumble and, hopefully, rise above the bad cycle they're in. Sometimes these people are as emotionally crippled and immature as babies. But just like babies, you have to put them down so they can learn to walk on their own. One day they might be able to run out the door, but whatever you do, do not crawl with them!!! Part of staying in your lane is encouraging those around you to be responsible for their individual journeys. Do not become a tow truck, dragging these people behind you. Otherwise you will always be in service and neglecting your own course of direction.

"The very time I thought I was lost, my dungeon shook and my chains fell off."
—JAMES BALDWIN

There Is Nothing Sweet About Bitter Friends

It took me quite awhile to get back into the dating game after my husband's death. My loss and pain were enormous, but the experience left me stronger and wiser going forward on my life's journey. When I finally took a stab at dating again, I was introduced to a gentleman who said that he had developed an aversion to dating women over forty because too often he found them to be jaded and angry. Or, if they weren't angry, they surrounded themselves with angry and bitter friends. He believed that toxic friends were standing in the way of happiness for many women. I have since heard the same lament from other men with whom I have had strictly platonic relationships, and I started to wonder whether there was any merit to this assessment. When litigants from dysfunctional families come before me in court I always tell them that they can't choose their family, but thank God they can choose their friends. Well, this applies to you and me also. And when we choose our friends, we need to make wise choices.

I believe that I have chosen some great friends. Becoming a judge and someone with a show on television has drawn many new people into my life. But I don't fret and worry about anyone's personal motives because I have learned to periodically check the air for negative energy and intentions. We all have to be vigilant about whom we welcome into our inner circle. It is our sanctuary and safe space. People are either in-laws or outlaws in my book. So, this is the question I ask myself when assessing people around me: Is this person motivating me to grow to be even better and brighter? If the answer is "no," then that person is relegated to the outlaw category and shown to the nearest door. I urge you to take the same drastic measures with anyone in your circle who does not have your highest good in mind and heart.

I am reminded of a *friend of a friend* named Samantha. Although I never said anything to my friend, Denise, I always wondered why she and Samantha were friends. Denise was so vivacious, charming, and full of life, and Samantha was such a sad sack. Then again, Denise was the type to befriend the friendless, so it wasn't such a stretch of the imagination that she would try to help Samantha. For years Denise and her husband had been trying to have a baby. They had everything going for them in life, including a great love story, but had never been blessed with children. Finally, she got pregnant with twins. I remember when she first told me the news. It was such a happy day. She and her husband were so excited and made all kinds of preparations for the babies' arrival. Her other friends and I threw a huge baby shower for her, and she received many useful gifts. We had a wonderful time sharing the joy of impending mother- hood with Denise at the shower. We played games and held contests like racing to see who could put a diaper on a baby doll the fastest. Another game was guessing how big and pregnant the mother-to-be was by using lengths of toilet paper. They were silly games for prizes, but a lot of fun. And all the women laughed and joked and ate except for one— Samantha. The entire time Samantha sat in a corner, not really participating and not showing any real signs of en- gagement, but just sitting apart gloomily. She didn't want to play any of the games. She said she felt like they were silly. Ordinarily this type of energy would cast such a negative mood throughout a room, but I guess our joy was just too powerful. It was one of the first baby showers I had ever at- tended, and I had a ball and left thinking what lucky and blessed children the twins were going to be.

Seven months into her pregnancy, Denise went into labor and the twins were stillborn. It was such a dark period for her. I remember the heaviness of the emotions we were all feeling at that time. Although I tried to put on a good face for Denise, the news almost paralyzed me. I could not begin to imagine the deep, deep sorrow she and her hus- band must have been feeling. All of a sudden, Samantha sprang into action. She was there in the hospital with Denise every day. When Denise was released from the hospital, not only was she depressed, but she was also bedridden because the trauma had taken a toll on her body. Samantha insisted on helping with the laundry, raking up leaves in the yard, making burial arrangements, taking Denise to doctor's appointments, and cooking meals for the family. It was like Samantha couldn't do enough for them, and everyone around said, "What a good friend that Samantha is!"

After a brief recovery period, Denise got pregnant again, and with only a couple of weeks left before the due date, it looked like everything was going to be all right with the new baby. One day Samantha came over to visit the expectant couple. I heard she looked like she had been drinking. Denise was in the baby's room decorating one of the walls with the pretty gift bags that her baby shower presents came in. Real cute! Samantha came in and sat in a rocking chair, rocking back and forth, quiet at first. Then, out of nowhere, she blurted: "Why is it that life is always so good to *you*? Huh? Why? You have a husband with a high-paying job who loves you, a great big beautiful house, and everybody knows you in your career. When you lost the twins I thought life had finally cut you down to size. Now you're ready to deliver a baby! Does your good luck never end?!" Denise told me her jaw dropped. She had never realized the envy this woman was harboring in her heart. It was surrounding Denise the entire time. Behind the smiles and the offers of help was a secret animosity and silent prayers for ill fortune to fall upon Denise and her family.

Bitter friends try to knock you off your path. Sometimes it's obvious. And sometimes it's seething in the darkness. But a whole lot of damage can be done in the dark. Generally speaking, it's sometimes hard to accept that not everybody you meet likes you. My grandmother always says, "You are not a hundred-dollar bill. Everybody likes hundred-dollar bills." A smiling face doesn't always mean that a person in your life is operating in your best interest. As I say to my family and the inner circle of friends I love, admire, and count on, choose YOUR friends wisely. You get just one life to live and it's *your* journey. Always think twice before you pick up hitchhikers. They can sometimes detour you from your intended route. And sometimes they're hiding daggers!

⊢━

"No person is your friend who demands your silence, or denies your right to grow."
—ALICE WALKER

Truths I Have Learned
About Children

The other day my brother and I visited some friends of his, a married couple who had just moved into a new house, so the chaos of boxes and packing materials greeted us at the door. They have a cute-as-a-button two-year-old daughter and are expecting their second child in a few months. The living room was full of toys. Dolls, musical instruments, games, puzzles, and stuffed animals were strewn about the room. We must have spent about an hour visiting this family. During the entire time, the little girl kept busy playing with a piece of bubble wrap! She never once picked up any of the numerous toys that her parents had showered her with. Her fancy was captured by something that cost absolutely nothing. The scene reminded me of a Christmas holiday that I had celebrated with family in my home.

As I mentioned in the introduction, I have ten nieces and nephews, and every other Christmas I host the holiday festivities at my house for my family and close friends. All the nieces and nephews receive gifts from the great- and grandparents and from their uncles and aunts. Well, this Christmas, my nieces and nephews ranged from ages four to thirteen. I knew that my other family members would buy them the video games, fancy cameras, and other popular and pricey trinkets kids play with these days. I thought about the many children around the world who were cold, hungry, or homeless during the holidays. The children in my family had a lot to be thankful for, and spending money on expensive gifts that year, and the years since then, did not seem right to me. That Christmas I decided I was not spending more than $10 on each child's gift. The only way to accomplish this goal was by shopping at a dollar store for toys. I was glad I had made this decision in early November, so the selection in the store had not yet been picked over. That year I bought marbles, a jump rope, a badminton set, a ping-pong set, a 750-piece jigsaw puzzle, and some other inexpensive toys.

I felt a bit of apprehension about the way the children would react to their presents. Maybe they would abandon the cheap gifts in the corner somewhere or complain outright about them. Well, let me tell you, those inexpensive toys that I gave them were the hit of Christmas that year.

After lunch, we set up the badminton game in the backyard and the whole family had a ball learning to play, even the grown-ups! I still have memories of looking outside and watching my mother skip rope as my two nieces turned it. The very next day, all the kids insisted on coming back over to my house so we could put together the jigsaw puzzle. We spent the entire day after Christmas eating popcorn and doing a puzzle together. All these years later, I still have that puzzle in my house.

When I later thought about why my family preferred these toys over the more expensive ones they received, I decided it was because those toys, though simple, challenged the mind and required more than one player. It confirmed something that I have always believed, which is that children inherently want to learn and prefer playing with others over playing alone. Children "think" they want the latest games and toys that the commercials tell them they need, but I am here to tell you from experience that those toys would gather dust on the shelf if children had playtime with family members. As children, my brothers, sisters, and I played many games together, such as Monopoly, Red Light/Green Light, Mother May I?, Go Fish, Concentration, and Trouble. I have fond memories of sitting around the table or running around the yard playing these games with my siblings.

More recently, in 2005, a tropical storm came through Miami and left a large portion of the city without lights. As fate would have it, my house was included in the grid of homes without electricity. No one among my friends and family had power in their houses either. With each day that passed, I resisted buying a generator because I was hoping that the electricity would be back on at any minute. Five days had passed and I was still without lights, and to my disappointment the hardware stores were sold out of generators. I was living alone at that time, so my fifteen-year-old niece, along with two of her schoolmates, offered to come over to stay with me at my house.

By the time the girls joined me, all the perishable food had done just that, perished without any refrigeration to preserve it. I was down to bottled water, peanut butter and jelly for sandwiches, and unhealthy snack foods like chips, cookies, and the Vienna sausages that I bought at a convenience store. That was the tasty diet we subsisted on—so much for hurricane preparedness. For news and updates, I had only an old battery-operated transistor radio my daddy had given me. During the day, it was hot outside and even hotter inside. Miami is a miserable place to be in the summer without air-conditioning. There seems to be at least one swimming pool per block. It is a standard feature for homes in this subtropical city. But once the electricity goes out, the pool pumps cannot filter the water and after about a day or two, the water turns green with algae. So this was my life in the summer of '05 in Miami.

Businesses and county offices were closed and for a time, a curfew had been imposed throughout the county. My days with the teenagers consisted of sitting around outside in swimsuits playing cards and board games, eating peanut butter and jelly sandwiches, listening to music on the transistor radio, and cooling off in the green water of the stagnant swimming pool. At night we lit candles in the living room and made up fairy tales as we laughed and fanned ourselves with newspapers and ate stale cookies and crackers. I was beginning to feel sorry for these girls: no cell phones, no hot water to bathe in, no cooked food to eat, no television or Internet. By a teenager's standards, it was a very primitive situation that we were in.

After a week of no electricity, we got news that power had been restored in my sister's neighborhood. Hallelujah!!! I offered to take the girls back home to a "civilized" environment, but they said they were worried about me and didn't want me to stay alone without power. I told them my grandmother and her cousin had had their power restored, and I would go stay with them until mine returned. They kept throwing out various arguments about why I should stay at my house. Then it dawned on me: they wanted to stay. And then they admitted that they weren't ready to go back to the creature comforts that they were used to, so we all stayed at my house and roughed it for another few days until the power came on!

As I look back on that time, I think that having no outside distractions allowed us to connect in ways that these children rarely got the chance to. Over that period of time they reconnected with their five senses—sight, touch, taste, hearing, and smell. In sports, they call it getting back to basics. Growing up in the early sixties my family never identified ourselves as being a rich family. We were fortunate to receive a valuable trinket here and there. Our riches came from knowing that we were loved by our parents and from the support and sharing we provided to each other through discussion and by looking into each other's eyes, holding on to each other's arms, and hearing the cadence of each other's voices as we talked about our lives and what was important to us. That's how families connected when I was growing up. That's how they built solid bonds. I cannot overstate the importance of taking time to talk and build relationships with those you love and care about. Especially the children in your life. Find out what's important to them, what you have in common, their likes and dislikes, their dreams for the future, how they feel about the neighbor down the street, what they're good at, what challenges their motor skills, what makes them sad and happy. During that power outage of 2005, my niece and I became closer and our bond stronger.

In today's society, relating well to one another is a lost art. I believe this is why so many lost and broken souls appear before me in court. They don't have that connection with family and humanity. That makes a person vulnerable to making wrong turns and their most regrettable mistakes. It's a fast-paced and often crazy world in which we live, and if you don't have the support and love of someone who thinks you matter, you will find yourself feeling lost and alone. These children gave me so much more than companionship during the outage. They also gave me the knowledge and insight that the core of who we are as a people has not changed—we all have the desire and need to connect with and relate to one another as we navigate and continue to change lanes in our efforts to appeal to our better angels. The core of who we are still exists as it did when we were growing up. What has changed, however, are the outside influences and, sadly, our inability to cope with them in a positive manner. The truth I've learned not only about children but from children is that we have to get back to basics. It's not about that which is expensive or extravagant, or the latest or best gadget, clothing item, car, or home. We have to get back to relating openly and honestly to one another, in our barest and most natural state, without outside interference and without ego. We have to sit down at the dinner table with our children, establish a family night when we talk or play games, and turn off the television and the computers at least one day a week and bake cookies and talk. Ask your children about their day and about their teachers and friends. Plan weekend outings to the library or museums or parks. How about just firing up the grill and having hot dogs on a Wednesday night? Being able to communicate with our children every day about what matters in their lives and about their dreams is a gift. Treasure that gift, because they will only be children once.

⊢—

"Your children need your presence more than your presents."
—JESSE JACKSON

You Need to Know Which Side of the Bread Your Butter Is On

As a young girl, whenever I would pitch a fit over the things that I didn't want to do but that were necessary for family harmony and progress, my mother would say, "You need to know what side of the bread your butter is on." To me this expression means knowing and understanding your role and what you want from your existence, knowing that you are in control of what is going on in your life. Ultimately, it means realizing what is advantageous to your self-growth and self-preservation.

In my thirteen years as a criminal defense attorney, I only had one client who fully understood this concept. David had been in and out of jail for many drug-related petty crimes and serious felonies. His mother said that no matter what the family did to get David on the right track—trips to church, stints in drug treatment centers, and aggressive interventions—David would end up using drugs and going to jail. On this particular occasion, David found himself on trial for an armed robbery that carried a life sentence. I was appointed by the court to represent David. When I visited David in jail to prepare for the trial, he steadfastly declared his innocence. David was terrified at the thought of being incarcerated for the rest of his life, and he revealed to me the most humiliating aspects of his life as a drug addict. He hated that his addictions had caused his mother many sleepless nights and took years off of her life as well as his own. He had lost respect for himself. His sincerity convinced me that David was telling the truth about his role in the robbery, and that something in him had changed during the short time I knew him.

We had a two-day trial. The judge charged the jury and sent it off to consider its verdict. As the jury returned to the courtroom, I felt a hollowness and anxiety in the pit of my stomach. I believed so much in the truth of David's account of the events and that he had truly found some redemption during the several months he had spent in jail awaiting trial. Then the clerk read the verdict: "Not Guilty." David was so overcome with joy that he grabbed me in a bear hug, and we both tumbled onto the floor in tears. David's mother told me that she knew that I had somehow saved her son's life. And, as with most of my past clients, David promised he would never be in trouble or in jail again. I wanted to believe him, but I was doubtful.

A few years ago, I was ordering burgers at a drive-through in an unfamiliar part of my city. As I was waiting for change, the manager came up to the window. It was David! He reached out the window to hug me, and then, with his face beaming, he drew up his sleeve to show me that he had "Karen" tattooed across his upper shoulder. He said that the trial had been the dividing line in his life. Ever since the acquittal, he quit drugs (on his own and without intervention!) and started working. I saw David again a few years later. I was vacationing in the Caribbean, and I saw him on the beach, this time accompanied by his wife and four children. He told me he owned a house and a successful business. There was a light beaming from inside of him that I can still remember to this day.

David's story really illustrates that in order for things to change and start working for us, we have to realize our own power to effect change. We have the power to fight off the negativity and pain that keep showing up on every corner. David started to realize that those momentary drug highs brought him back down into the same dead-end life, day after day. He was tired of living in fear and addiction, and he wasn't getting anything constructive from being a drug addict. He had a family and a God who he realized loved him unconditionally. He stopped playing the role of the miserable victim of his addictions and took on the role of victor. He started operating from strength and courage. He finally realized which side of the bread his butter was on.

I think it's a shame some of us have to learn from personal experience when it is so much easier and a lot less painful to learn from the mistakes of others. David had to nearly lose his liberty to learn what was important, real, and essential for a life of quality. Weathering bad storms can make us stronger and wiser. I say all the time, "For my journey, I can withstand hurricane-force winds." Nothing can protect us from life: the good, the bad, and the ugly of it. Coming out unharmed on the other side of the bad and the ugly can leave us with valuable information to prepare for the next bump in the road ahead. Do *you* know what side of the bread your butter is on?

⊢

"The only real mistake is the one from which we learn nothing."
–JOHN POWELL

"Mother" Is a Verb!

We've all heard the idiom *actions speak louder than words*. We all learned in grade school that a noun, among other things, is a person, place, or thing. A name. But a verb denotes action. And so it is the with the verb "mother." Just about anybody who is fertile can be *a mother,* the noun. But it takes a true commitment to the growth and well-being of the child you produce *to mother* it. Unless you demonstrate through action your love, commitment, and dependability in performing the duty of mothering, you are a mother in name only. In my twenty-year legal career I have come into contact with many lost souls. The most poignant of them suffer from a lack of mothering, and fathering, and all of its implications. I am well aware of the alarming numbers of absent fathers in many children's lives. But I am calling on mothers here because only women can bear children. To constantly blame what's wrong with your child on his absent father keeps you and your child in the position of being victims of circumstances. I want to help you transform yourself into a victor over circumstances!

It is rare to find a person who has fallen into the legal system who has not been the product of an appalling childhood. One of my very first clients was a woman named Valerie. She started out life in a good home with a loving family. Her mother was a teacher, and her dad a cop. Actually, I recall that she told me that her father was the first black police chief in their city. He died when Valerie was five or six, and her mother quickly remarried a much younger man who never kept a job. Valerie was the only girl in a family with two boys. She had done very well in school, so well that she won a full scholarship to a prestigious university, the largest nonathletic scholarship the university had ever awarded. She graduated near the top of her class and afterward accepted a great job offer back in her hometown and found herself an apartment.

Soon after settling into adult life, something happened to Valerie. She stopped showing up at work. She stopped bathing herself. She stopped talking to her friends. She had become a cocaine addict. Eventually, she lost her job and her apartment and took to living on the streets. Despite the intervention of friends and family, Valerie was always back

out on the streets in an endless hunt for the rock—crack cocaine that she could smoke from a pipe. She had a two-page
rap sheet of petty offenses. Her case came to me after she
was arrested inside a crack house. Police found her there,
nine months pregnant, on her knees performing oral sex on
a man and his teenage son. All for a five-dollar hit.

Valerie looked nothing like her twenty-five years. She
had grown hard, and there was no light behind her eyes. I
asked her how she had ended up living such a sordid life.
She said that early in her childhood, she had had the love
and nurturing of two parents. She was especially close to her
father. She hardly had time to mourn his passing before her
mother brought another man into the home to replace him.
This man initiated her into sex at twelve and introduced her
to drugs when she was fourteen years old. What hurt Valerie
the most was that her mother knew what was going on. She
had also known that the man had a prior conviction for rape
before she married him. Yet, she chose to share her bed and
her daughter's virtue with a man who had shown no respect
at all for women by committing the worst crime against
them. Valerie said she never felt safe. She walked through
her life in a constant state of fear. I believe that the first place
we learn safety is in the bosom of our home. We eventually
learn that the world can be a dangerous place, but we can always find comfort when we reach the door to that place we
call home. It wasn't there for Valerie. The inside world of her
home was just as dangerous as the outside world. So she
threw herself into schoolwork and after-school activities to

avoid having to go home. Her hard work paid off in the scholarship, but she was always searching for peace of mind, searching for a place of refuge and comfort. Eventually she found it at the end of a crack pipe.

If I had a hundred dollars for every time I have come across this type of story, I would have been a rich woman a long time ago. Only 10 percent of girls who are sexually abused are abused by strangers; the other 90 percent are raped by someone they know and trust. Additionally, one in four girls has been sexually abused before the age of seventeen.* I work with a lot of girls in the courts and in the juvenile and foster care system and I have yet to meet one who did not come from a home where she was raped by a boyfriend or husband of the mother. One child I know was abandoned by her mother *and* grandmother when she reported that her father had been raping her since she was five. She has been a ward of the state of Florida, in and out of foster homes, ever since.

I could fill this section with story upon story of young women who have appeared before me in court and elsewhere who come from homes where men were allowed sexual freedom with them. I always ask them, "Where was your mother? What was she doing to protect you?" I am not hating on men here. I happen to come from a home with a loving and protective father. And while drug addiction and prison time have touched my family, my own male care-

---

*Kilpatrick, D., Saunders, B., & Smith, D. *Youth Victimization: Prevalence and Implications.* U.S. Department of Justice, National Institute of Justice Report (2003)

givers were honorable and exemplified manhood in my eyes. But the truth is, the vast majority of rape and violence against women in America is perpetrated by men.

Part of staying in your lane is being responsible and standing to answer for the choices you make in life. If you make the decision to have children, then you must also accept the attendant responsibilities that go along with that decision. No one puts a gun to your heads and says "give birth." It is a matter of choice. But motherhood is not a job for the faint of heart or for those with low self-esteem. If you have low self-esteem, you will keep looking outside of yourself for someone to give value to you, and often that someone will be a man. Sometimes we become blinded by our need to couple, our need for affection, our need for love. It is one thing to have that need on your own; it is quite another to throw children into the mix. Anybody can be a mother. It takes a self-possessed woman *to mother.*

If your having children was a mistake, mother them well anyway. If your having children has prevented you from having romantic love in your life, mother them well anyway. And if you do not have the skills to mother the child you have produced, then it is your duty to seek help and guidance. Staying in your lane means owning up to every consequence of the choices you make in this life. That includes the choice to become a mother. No excuses are acceptable here. If you have chosen to have children, then choose to make their future *your* responsibility. No one else's. If your child has a good father, that's the icing on the cake. But it's ultimately your cake.

"There is no way to be a perfect mother, and a million ways to be a good one."

–JILL CHURCHILL

Baby Drama

D r. King said "our lives begin to end the day we become silent about things that matter." I refuse to keep silent about this subject. It may not be well embraced or politically correct, but I feel that it's important to shoot as straight as an arrow because, truthfully, so many innocent lives are at risk of being woefully damaged that I personally rank this subject on par with a national disaster. The title of this chapter could easily be called, "What is happening to baby?" or "What's wrong with my baby?" but in the end it really is about baby drama—the attitudes and irrational actions of parents, both maternal and paternal, who have not operated from love in terms of doing what's right for their child. They have chosen instead to do what serves their personal interest, regardless of the outcome, and baby be damned!

What I have to say here is not based on hearsay, gossip, popular culture, or urban legend. It is based on common sense, and I could have written this entire book solely about baby drama. When I see parents acting out baby drama I see dysfunction, insecurity, immaturity, and lives filled with nothing but selfish motives. I tell people all the time that life is like a game of cards and we are dealt a hand. And while some hands are more difficult to play than others, in the end, after we've studied the hand we've been dealt and surveyed the table, looking dead into the eyes of those who want to defeat us (I take a game of cards very seriously), it comes down to how we choose to play our hand that counts. The game of life is about calculated choices too. We choose how we live our lives! So let's be very clear here. If you know that the way you've chosen to play your hand has led to a life of financial instability, or a life out of control, or a life where there is rain and clouds and very little sun, then why bring a child into such a crazy, mixed-up situation? I am talking to women here. Only a woman can bear a child, so you are ultimately the one in the position of power. And with that power comes responsibility.

A child is a gift, not a saving grace to a marriage that had no foundation to build on from the beginning. A child is a blessing, not a meal ticket to a better standard of living or something you create and then turn your back on for a lifetime. A child is a miracle, not a doll, or pawn, or assurance against loneliness. There are many incredible and wonderful reasons to have children. But if your reason is not honorable, then you have set yourself and your child up for dysfunction and disappointment. It's hard enough raising a child under the best of circumstances, but when you inject the wrong reasons for conception into the conversation you're already adding to your burden and to the increased probability that your child will receive the same type of hand you were dealt.

I have adjudicated countless child-support and custody matters. I have seen and heard it all before. Dad shows up to pick up baby at his court-ordered visitation time, and no one is home; mom drops off two-month-old baby with dad for visitation without food, bottles, clothing, or diapers; mom refuses to allow dad visitation because she does not trust his new wife or girlfriend; mom tells kid what a low-down rotten scoundrel dad is (what does that say about mom's choices?); mom leaves town or the country with baby without dad's approval or knowledge (after all, she's "my baby"); dad drills kid with questions after every visitation with mom to find out who mom is dating now; mom denies dad visitation because dad is late or not paying child support; dad refuses to pay child support because he thinks mom spends the money on cars and luxury items; dad ignores or neglects his child because he wants to keep his new wife happy. In each of these scenarios and the hundreds of others out there, the child is being used to send a message. No one is thinking about what the little messenger is feeling or thinking, or how their actions today will negatively impact the child's actions tomorrow.

When I was in private practice, I was appointed by the court to be the guardian ad litem for a twelve-year-old boy in the middle of a visitation/child support battle. A guardian ad litem represents the child and makes recommendations to the court based on the child's best interest. In this particular case the mother, Marisa, had a brief affair with a pizza chain owner named Carlo. When she became pregnant, he told her that he wasn't going to marry her. Number one, he was already married. And number two, he had fifteen other children by various women. All girls. Surprisingly, he did pay child support for all of them. I bet he had to bake a lot of pizzas to meet his obligations, but he did it. Marisa thought that the fact that she was bearing a son would be the catalyst to get him to leave his wife once and for all, marry her, and stay faithful. Carlo had always wanted a son, but this alone wasn't enough for him to completely abandon his long-suffering wife and commit to Marisa.

After their son was born, Marisa never sought child support because she knew that Carlo would then demand visitation. She spent the next twelve years moving with the boy from city to city in an effort to prevent him from having contact with his father. When she moved back to South Florida, Carlo found out and brought a paternity action suit, which is how they wound up in court. The first time the father ever laid eyes on his son was at the hearing where I was appointed. Marisa was adamant that the father should not have visitation. She was extremely hostile and bitter about Carlo, even though she had not seen him in twelve years. She argued that visitation would psychologically damage the boy, that he would be confused by having to spend whole weekends with this man he did not know. She even accused Carlo of being an unfit father because he had so many children by so many different women. I remember wanting to say: Didn't you think of that when you got pregnant? When I first met Marisa she was crying hysterically outside the courtroom as her lawyer tried to explain to her that there was no legal basis to prevent a father and son relationship.

On the day I was appointed as the guardian for the child, J.R., I interviewed him in a private conference room in the courthouse. My first impression was that he looked terrified. He was a skinny, shy boy who wore a dark suit much too big for his frame. I introduced myself and explained that I would be making a recommendation to the judge about visitation based on our interviews. He looked down at his hands most of the time as I asked him questions. When I asked him how he felt about visitation with his dad, he was quiet at first. I didn't know what he was going to say. I was thirty years old and had very little experience in family court matters at that time. I felt certain that he would echo the bitterness and resentment I was sure he had heard from his mother for the past twelve years. He said to me very softly, almost in a whisper, "Will you promise not to say that I said this?" He told me that he had dreamed every night for as long as he could remember about meeting his dad. He said he loved his mom and he didn't want to hurt her. But he wanted to be around the man who was his dad. Seeing his dad for the first time in court made him long even more for a father/son bond. He wanted to do the things that boys do with their dads. Nothing grandiose, just simple things like going to the barbershop for a haircut or watching a basketball game on TV together. He told me he also needed his dad to show him how to tie a necktie. When he pulled the clip-on tie off of his neck, we both laughed for the first time.

That experience was my first realization that boys need their dads or father figures in ways women can't understand. It's the same way girls need mother figures in ways men can't understand. This boy, who had been mothered for his entire life, was yearning for the chance to be fathered. Luckily, the lawyers and I were able to work out an agreement without having a full hearing. Carlo and J.R. were given a visitation schedule. Fast forward fifteen years or so. I was having lunch with a friend in an Italian restaurant in downtown Miami when the manager came up to me. It was J.R. He told me that he and his father had expanded from pizza parlors into restaurants and now owned businesses in the next county as well. I guess that psychological damage that the mother insisted would occur from the relationship backfired on her because not only did J.R. survive, he thrived!

There is no guarantee in life that any two people who come together to conceive a child will live happily ever after. What I have witnessed in court many times is women who feel that their child is an insurance policy that will keep the man in their lives forever. For this reason, women often end up disappointed and disillusioned because they think that if they have a baby with Jerry, it will make Jerry stay around. But the problems in the relationship started long before baby, and therefore will not get fixed just because baby has been introduced into the equation. Then the same mothers decide to have yet another baby with the next love interest in the hopes that this time will be different. This man will be different. The cycle just continues. Unless you have a ball and chain to hold him down, there is no way that you can make someone stay with you forever, no matter how many children you have.

I've also seen one parent using a child as a weapon of mass destruction against the other, "offending" parent. One parent may not be able to control the other, but he or she can definitely control whether the other parent sees the child on the weekends, celebrates the child's birthday, attends the child's football game, or, fill in the blank. I have to admit, the vast majority of the time that I have seen this activity, it's been perpetuated by women who have primary custody of their children. I have actually taken custody away from mothers who play these games with the father and the court. I have had many private discussions in my chambers with young children. Countless times I have ended up rocking a child in my arms who was in tears because of parental fights and recriminations. Baby drama. I have cried with them and for them. If you really think the child's other parent is a hateful good-for-nothing, then what does that say about you choosing a hateful good-for-nothing to lie down with?

When I was calling my domestic violence docket in Hialeah, Florida, in 2007, I came across a couple from the Middle East who had four children. The mother of these children was seeking a restraining order against the father for physical and psychological abuse. She indicated that she was not allowed to work and was forced to perform sexual favors for her husband in order to get money to buy the most basic necessities. He treated her like a slave whose function was to produce babies, keep house, and have sex with him whenever and wherever he demanded it. She was not very familiar with U.S. customs, and a neighbor who overheard the woman being beaten knocked on this woman's door and gave her information about going into a domestic violence shelter with her children. This kind neighbor actually helped the woman pack up her kids and drove her to the shelter. Once at the shelter, the staff there helped the woman file an affidavit for a restraining order.

During the first court hearing, the husband testified that his wife was lying. He had never allowed her to seek U.S. citizenship, and now, he said, he was making the necessary preparations to take the entire family back home to their country. He said that his wife was changing. She was no longer listening to him, and was being influenced negatively by American ways. Without shame, he told me that American women have too much freedom and too many rights, and he no longer wanted his family to be a part of such corruption. After hearing testimony from the neighbor and looking at photos of the woman's bruises taken by administrators at the shelter, I entered a restraining order and awarded temporary custody of the children to the wife pending further investigation. By his own design and desire, the husband had been the sole provider for the family. Therefore, I ordered him to pay child support, but I did not make a decision on the issue of spousal support until further investigation. Well, he told me right then and there that he was not going to pay a dime. If she wanted her freedom, then she would have to find a way to support herself *and* the kids. I told him that I was resetting the case in three weeks for a report on whether he had followed the court instructions. He said he understood that if he had not paid support, he was going to jail for contempt of court.

In the intervening three weeks, one of my clerks came to my chambers with a police report on another incident involving this family. I thought the husband had found out where his wife and kids were living and violated the restraining order in some way. But it was worse news. Apparently, one of the children had contracted whooping cough and died in the hospital. I remember feeling awful about the implications of this new twist in the case. Now the husband could argue that the wife was unfit to have custody of the remaining kids, and the wife would feel that she was being punished by God for having disobeyed her husband. That is exactly what I thought.

The day came for the report in court. When I took my seat at the bench, I saw the husband sitting in the back row of the courtroom with his arms folded across his chest.

When I called the case, both parties walked up to their respective podiums. I didn't even have to ask about the child support. The husband was carrying his suitcase. I had the bailiff take him straight into custody, and I sentenced him to sixty days in jail for contempt. He said: "I don't care if I rot in jail, I am not paying one dime. She'll see, she can't make it without my help." He seemed solid in his resolve. I told him that he could purge himself of the contempt and get released from jail whenever he decided to abide by the court order and pay the support. Do you know that he spent sixty days in jail without making a single attempt to pay? That is just how intent he was on controlling his wife and making her and the kids suffer.

When the case came up for final hearing, it was obvious that no amount of jail time would make the husband pay support for his kids. But rather than appearing defeated, his wife looked stronger than I had ever seen her. She said the grief from the death of her child demonstrated to her that she had more strength than she had ever known. She was still living in the shelter but was now working two jobs. "I have my own money now. The kids and I will make it here in this country." It made my heart feel good that one monkey didn't stop her show.

I make no apologies about the fact that I am passionate about the well-being of children and how the actions of those to whom their lives have been entrusted mold and shape these future citizens of the world. What we are exposing some of them to would have been grounds for child abuse charges decades ago. None of us have a choice in the type of family environment we're born into any more than we have a choice in the color of our eyes, or race, or economic class. But, absent religious or cultural conviction, the choice to have a child is in our realm of control, and people have to start making that decision wisely.

Any way you look at it, having a child is a big deal, and you will have to make enormous sacrifices as well as undergo an honest assessment of where you are in your life at that particular moment in time. Couple that with the fact that you will be sharing your DNA with a partner who will, through blood if nothing else, be part of this child's life for the rest of its life. Some of the people who come before me in court and who I meet in everyday life take more time to choose the outfit they are wearing than they do in deliberating the important decisions around whether or not to have a child. They need to ask such questions as: Am I willing to share my DNA profile with this person lying next to me? Will he/she be a good parent to our child? Has he/she been good to me in this relationship? Has he/she been a good parent to their other children? Have I known this person long enough to know his/her true character? Am I in a stable emotional and financial position to raise this child by myself if it comes to that? As I have said before, I place more responsibility on women because only women can have children, so we have the upper hand in the area of deciding to have kids.

As for men, I am tired of hearing "she tricked me," "I

didn't know she was psychotic," "she should have known it meant nothing to me." You have as much responsibility toward the child as the mother does. None of these excuses, from men or from women, mean a hill of beans when you have both created another living being who needs love, protection, and nurturing for nearly two decades.

I know life isn't perfect, which I've said over and over again. But come on, we have to do better than we have been doing, because the future of our children is at stake! When you do what you've always done, you get what you've always gotten. And let's just look at what we've been getting—babies are having babies, crime among twelve- to twenty-four-year-olds is higher than any other group in the U.S., the number of children in foster care has grown exponentially, the dropout rate in schools in this country is at an all-time high, and the list goes on and on. There is a correlation between how a child is raised and how a child conducts himself in society. It's a proven fact. We look at these children and we shake our heads in disgust, but somebody somewhere brought them to this point. Children come into the world like a blank canvas, and it is the parent's responsibility to paint a picture that will serve their children throughout their lives. Children come into the world innocent and trusting, and they see the truth and value in the world. Children are not born to hate, or be racist, or even to be cynical or apathetic. All that they are or will ever be depends upon you, as parents, coming together to provide them a healthy and wholesome environment in which to grow up. Allow that growth to take place in your child with both parents giving a double dose of love, guidance, and direction. Learn to play fair now, or pay for it later. As with everything you do, it's your choice.

—

"The person who complains about the way the ball bounces is likely to be the one who dropped it."
–Lou Holtz

Only Adults Have a Right to Privacy

I was sitting in my chambers one day during my first few months as a judge when I heard a knock on my door. It was a clerk asking if I was free to perform a marriage ceremony. In Florida, parties may have civil marriages performed in the courthouse by a sitting judge. I was so excited. This would be my first marriage ceremony. My well-known burgundy robe is one of several that I wear on the bench, but that day I chose to wear my "formal" robe in the traditional black with velvet panels in the front. I put it on, grabbed my Bible, and headed downstairs to the wedding chapel in the office of the county clerk.

When I walked into the chapel, the room was full of people, but the mood did not feel festive. I expected the excitement that surrounds a wedding ceremony, but it felt more like a funeral. There were several adults present, three or four babies and toddlers, and two teenagers. I asked the clerk to identify the bridal couple. She then called up the two teenagers! The girl had just cele-brated her sixteenth birthday and the boy was seventeen. Both were grade school dropouts. I later learned they had two children already. I thought they were too young to get married, but the clerk told me that the parents had con-sented to the union. I walked back upstairs to my chambers to review the Florida statutes on marriage and found that in Florida, a child fifteen or younger can only marry by order of a judge. However, a child sixteen or seventeen may marry with the consent of the parents. So I learned that only their parents could object to the union—not me! Although I had objections to the marriage, the law gave the parents the au-thority to consent to it. So, reluctantly I performed the cere-mony. My very first marriage ceremony, and I was signing the marriage certificate with sadness.

About three or four years later, I volunteered to hear do-mestic violence cases in a satellite courthouse. I called up a case where the wife alleged several acts of emotional and physical violence by her husband. After hearing testimony from her, I turned to the husband to hear his side of the story. His first words were "Judge, you married us." There they were in front of me on a domestic violence case: the first couple I had married. I learned that the wife was twelve years old when they started dating, and her boyfriend was often allowed to spend nights in her bedroom with the full knowledge of her parents. Soon, they had two babies and stopped going to school. The woman's mother was standing next to her in the courtroom. I asked her why she let her daughter have a boyfriend while she was still only a young child. Her mother answered, "I didn't want to get involved in her private life." I nearly fell out of my seat! What judgment had the parents shown in allowing these children that type of freedom and decision-making in the seventh grade? I did not see where they had faithfully accepted and exercised their duties as parents.

Children are entitled to alone time. Children are entitled to be loved and treated with respect. *But minor children do not have a right to privacy.* Yes, I said it and I stand firmly behind it! They rely on adults for their most basic needs. They do not have the means to feed, clothe, and house themselves. They have no right to vote, bear arms, or drive an automobile. They can't even register themselves for school. In short, they are ill-equipped to raise *themselves*. As long as your child is listed as a "dependent" on your tax return, you have a right to know what is going on in their world. Yes, you do. And it's not about watching them, it's about *watching out* for them.

How many times have you heard the news of some child who brought a firearm to school, whom police later learned had kept a small arsenal of firearms at home, right under the noses of the parents? I guess the parents didn't feel like they could just go barging into their child's rooms uninvited. If you don't know what your child is doing behind the closed doors of his or her bedroom or what he or she is doing on the Internet, then you are not being a parent. You are not raising a child. You are just being a landlord to a nonpaying tenant.

I hear so much about the dismal future of our youth. But, through my experiences on the bench, I have come to the conclusion that many parents are simply not rearing their children. We give our children too much: too much entertainment, too much food, too much freedom, and nowhere near enough parenting. Whose fault is that? It is the parents'! No one is more responsible for what is going right or wrong with your child than you are. The television, computers, and electronic games are not a substitute for a mother or father. Over the years I've come to realize that this is not a new phenomenon. I have often wondered what type of parent could allow their babies to share their bodies with a lover, drink with their buddies, or smoke marijuana under their roofs. When I question parents who allow this type of behavior, they often say that their son or daughter is "going to do it anyway so I'd rather they do it under my roof where I know they're safe." I've never understood this mentality. What happened to setting an example? Many parents have lost their way and have forgotten that they are the parents. You are not your child's friend. Even the best friend in the world isn't going to change our diapers, or potty train us, or sacrifice their life for us, or discipline us, or shape us into responsible adults. That is not a friend's job. That is your job.

I'm sick and tired of seeing lost and hurt children. I see them begging for money at gas stations. I see them lying on cold cement floors in jail waiting for a family member who never comes. I see them crying for their mothers and families while they languish in foster homes. I see them getting into the cars of strangers in the red-light district.

You *can* be a better parent. Did you have good parents yourself? If so, you should incorporate some of their parental skills for raising your own children. Are there other parents with well-adjusted kids whom you know? Talk to them about their parenting skills and techniques. You can read books on parenting or take courses. From my own experience, children learn discipline through having rules. Listen, we all live by rules as a society. There are rules of conduct, rules for operating a vehicle, rules for renovating your property, rules for the workplace, rules for buying a house, rules for owning a pet, and hundreds of other rules. So don't be put off by the word "rules." You have a right to know where your child is twenty-four hours a day. Set the rules. You have a right to know which websites your child visits. Set the rules. You have a right to limit television, check homework, and set a "lights out" time for going to bed. Set the rules!

Being a parent and directing your child's course right along with your own helps you live your best life. If your daughter becomes a baby factory, constantly needing to rely on you for support, then how can you live your best life? If your son never learns right from wrong and ends up spending his life in prison, how can you live your best life? If your child never learns independence and has to live with you for the rest of his life, how can you live your best life? It is up to you to take full control of the wheel with baby on board, directing both of your paths onto a better and brighter course. You owe that to yourself and to your child.

——

"The child supplies the power but the parents have to do the steering."

–Dr. Benjamin Spock

Pain Is the Hurt That Keeps on Giving

In 1999, I experienced the violent and unexpected death of my husband. The grief I was left with felt like being run off the road by an eighteen-wheeler and landing in a ditch on a dark and lonely stretch of road. And what an unfamiliar road it was. I had to learn a whole new landscape. It was during this time that I discovered that "life" is the thing that happens when we're making other plans. And in order to navigate its many twist and turns, we have to develop the emotional and spiritual agility to switch from plan a to plan b, and sometimes c or d. But once you have survived life's many pitfalls, you can emerge much stronger and wiser. I know I have.

My mother "mothered" me during my painful period of mourning. She forced me back into regularly performing the most basic, everyday functions like eating or bathing, in subtle and often not-so-subtle ways. All the while, she was urging me to get back into the game of life. At her suggestion, I attended a support group in my city for people who were dealing with the death of a loved one. I didn't really want to go, but I went at the gentle urging of my mother. I felt like I was one of the walking dead. Blood was flowing through my veins, but my spirit, my energy, my character, were all dead. I remember sitting outside the community center where the meetings were held, lost in a fog as I waited for the meeting to begin. A woman in her mid-fifties sat next to me, introduced herself, and welcomed me to the gathering. I usually enjoy meeting people and am quite a talkative person, but during that dark time, I could sit for hours without uttering a word, and I had none for her. As others arrived, she began to tell me her story.

She told me that fifteen years earlier, she and her husband of many years had owned and operated a family business, but were having problems with the IRS. They had been informed that that they would have to submit to an IRS audit. The couple disputed the claim of taxes owed and had been busy for weeks collecting the documentation for the audit. It was a tough process, but they were working as a team to get through it. The day of the audit, she and her husband met with an IRS tax examiner in their living room. The auditor spent time going over their paperwork and asked some questions about money the business had received that this lady knew nothing about. Her husband said he had some more supporting documentation in his upstairs office and excused himself to retrieve it. As she sat downstairs with the auditor, they heard a loud bang. They rushed upstairs and found her husband in his office slumped over at his desk, dead from a self-inflicted gunshot wound to the head. Can you imagine?

This woman was in total shock and disbelief. Her husband had left her, just like that. He had simply checked out. But even worse, he left a suicide note in which he blamed her for everything. Every problem and shortcoming in his life was her fault, including the tax issue. But the most egregious admonishment was that she was the reason he had killed himself. It was clear by the length of the note (it went on for five pages and had been typed) that he had planned this suicide all along. Who could fathom her grief? She told me that she put the letter in her dresser drawer and over the next several years, she *tortured* herself by pulling out that letter and ingesting its hurtful words over and over again.

Even as I struggled with my own grief, I remember my heart going out to that woman for the emotional hell she had endured. She said that she spent a great deal of time putting herself down and blaming herself for his demise. She spent hours questioning her value as a human being...as a wife...as a woman. She told me that it took her *years* to realize that she was not the reason for her husband's demise. His decision had been a result of his very own feelings of inadequacy. In retrospect, she realized that he had never really been a happy man. His mother died shortly after his birth, and his father remarried soon after and left him in the care of a distant relative who made him feel like a charity case. He was an abandoned and hurt little boy walking around in a grown man's clothes. Now, fifteen years after the tragedy, this woman had remarried and came to the support group to try to help others dealing with grief.

I recall another woman I met years ago. She was very quiet and diminutive, and her eyes had the look of the women in those black-and-white photos of farmers and their families during the Great Depression. Have you seen people like that before? People whose eyes are so weighted with sorrow, it's as though sadness fills up every nook and cranny of their souls. Their eyes always look like they are brimming with tears. Something makes me want to cry when I see people with those eyes. Well, Cleo had eyes like that. She had grown up in a tumultuous household run by alcoholics. Dinnertime with her drunken parents became a roundtable of put-downs for Cleo and her brothers. Cleo's home environment was a living hell full of cursing, tirades, violence, and sometimes rape at the hands of her father. To this day, Cleo says, she cringes whenever she hears the words "happy hour." She became addicted to prescription drugs for a while, but gave them up when she learned that she was pregnant with her first and only child. And despite her best intentions, she found herself verbally victimizing her son in the same fashion as her parents had done to her. She attacked his every move. When he didn't wash his hands, he was dirty. When he did wash his hands, he was wasting water. At some point, when the boy was around five, Cleo came to the realization that she was a "dry drunk," a person who keeps acting out the crazy and destructive behavior of an addict even though he or she has physically given up drinking or using drugs. But bless Cleo, she had enough sense to realize that she was damaging her child. She sent him to live with his father while she worked on herself mentally and emotionally. I applaud her for loving her child enough to send him to an environment that was emotionally healthier than the one she could provide. Today her son is a brilliant and healthy young man with a promising future.

People who are feeling pain on the inside can cause a lot of damage to their family and friends. It might be our parents who tell us we will never amount to anything because they heard the same words from their own parents. Or teachers, friends, or bosses who may have something in their past that tells them it is all right to spit on others the way they have been spat on. The trick is to realize that if that person had love, support, and guidance on his or her journey, they would not be spewing venom at the world, and that the pain they are inflicting on you is really a reflection of how they see themselves.

The stories of these two women represent the difference between owning up to the pain that we cause versus recognizing the pain that is not our fault. In order to heal we must see and know the difference. If we are the ones inflicting harm, then the challenge is to own up to what we are doing and stop it. Most people cannot see the ways in which they are harming those they love. You may be in denial. Here is where you have to rely on what your well-meaning friends and family may be telling you. Like a friend of mine says, "You can't see the back of your head." If you have friends and family who you know have your back, then you have to trust them if they are telling you that you are saying and doing things that are harming or hurting others.

The challenge for those on the receiving end of another's emotional, spiritual, or physical pain is to deploy your own natural defense mechanisms. It is easy for your defenses to get neutralized because your fear may be so great. There are organizations out there ready to provide you housing, food, legal representation, and counseling if you need it. You do not need to be held hostage to someone else's pain any longer.

To lead a life of purpose and self-respect, we must learn to put ourselves first in our own lives. We have to recognize and separate our own "stuff" from that of lovers and others who are keeping us sidetracked. We are the stars of this show called "My Life," and sometimes the supporting characters have to be replaced or written out of the script altogether. When you are about to take off on an airplane, the in-flight staff tells you, "In case we lose oxygen, put a mask on yourself first, then put one on your child." The same applies to other situations in which our own lives are threatened. We must take action to ensure our own survival. If you are living with or dating someone who is hurting you, your obligation is to protect yourself as you would against an enemy. You also need to realize when you are the enemy. Seek the help you need. There are plenty of organizations and groups ready to help you.

━

"It is not what you are called, but what you answer to."
—AFRICAN PROVERB

You Reap What You Sow

The saying "You reap what you sow" comes from Paul's letter to the Galatians in the New Testament. In the letter he wrote, "Whatsoever a man soweth, that he shall also reap." Simply stated the quote means that actions have consequences. I believe in the truth of this statement. Where you find yourself in the future is a direct result of what you have done in the past. I generally believe that when your intentions are good, and your motivation is not to harm but to uplift either yourself or someone else, the actions you take are laying the groundwork for a positive outcome.

Intuitively, each of us understands the idea that what we sow in life will ultimately be what we receive. Sometimes it's hard to focus on our goals because life throws a lot at us, and priorities can get lost along the way. However, it is because life throws so much at us that we must be ever vigilant in focusing on our goals, and, frankly speaking, some of us do it better than others. A few years ago I met two women, Lila and Shawn, who grew up next-door neighbors and became very good friends. These two women are the same race and age. They were both raised in single-parent households in the same rough Chicago neighborhood. They attended the same middle school and high school. Neither one of them had a positive role model in their mother, and neither of them had a father in the household. Both got pregnant at fifteen years old and dropped out of school in the tenth grade. This is such a common story. But that is where the paths of Lila and Shawn branched off from each other.

The father of Lila's child left her alone to raise their son. Her family bad-mouthed her for getting pregnant and even tried to convince her to put him up for adoption. But Lila was determined that, despite the lack of support and encouragement around her, she was not going to be another teenage mother statistic. She knew the odds were stacked a mile high against her. But she also knew she had to have a plan to pave a road out of the poverty and stagnation of the community where they lived. She came up with a plan to ensure her son's safety and education. Knowing that she couldn't provide a father for little Jake, Lila decided that she had to learn to be both a mother *and* a father. She had to be both compassionate and firm, so she resisted the temptation to coddle him, yet at the same time she wasn't a drill sergeant. Throughout his childhood, everything she did was for him, but she made sure her life was never all about him. Lila said she watched her own mother fail to find a balance between her child and a social life. Lila was determined to learn from those mistakes. Lila never knew her own father, and her mother paraded men in and out of her life and home. Her mother gave the men in her life priority over Lila. Though her son was important and she still had relationships with men, Lila never brought men around her son. She saw too often that women in her community would bring men into their homes, and the boys would grow attached to them. When the men would move on, they left the boys heartbroken. She didn't want to do that to her son.

Lila put Jake in the local police athletic league from age six to eleven. She pushed him to complete tasks even when he didn't want to. She encouraged him in athletics, but she stressed academics. She explained to him that there are fewer than 400 NBA players, but more than 50,000 lawyers in the world and told him that he could either be a ball player or a lawyer, but the odds were better for becoming a lawyer. She had to force him to complete his homework, go to school, and participate in baseball practice. She did this because she cared about her son and loved him. She knew the importance of his being dedicated to something. "I didn't want him to end up like the other loser boys on our block," she said. Lila went to school at night to get her GED while she worked full-time and sometimes part-time jobs to support them. She didn't get any help from her family or the government. She was a hostess in a restaurant, receptionist in a dental office, and sales clerk in a clothing store.

One day coming home from a double shift, Lila saw a group of young boys on their knees gambling with dice. Her first thought was, "Oh, no, that's not Jake ... I know that's not Jake!" Apprehensively she neared the stoop, only to find that her son was one of the boys throwing dice. She excused him from the group, and when they were in private she laid into him. "I know you can't help but hang out with those boys downstairs because they are around us, but if you become one of them, you will be a boy who isn't going anywhere and stuck in this neighborhood forever. You need to learn to be *with* them, but not *of* them," Lila scolded. She lived in a neighborhood where there were a lot of gunfights and drive-by shootings. Lila would always pray, "Please God, I don't want that to be my son's lot in life." When Jake finished middle school, Lila had a specific high school in mind for him. There was a very good private school in the city that was known for its structure and discipline. The government subsidized the school's tuition, but it was still very expensive and most parents couldn't afford the six-hundred-dollar-a-month fee. Lila scraped up the money, ate cheese sandwiches for dinner, and cut out unnecessary expenses. Jake was salutatorian of his high school class and was awarded a four-year academic scholarship at a prestigious college in Pennsylvania. He plans to attend Colombia University's Graduate School of Business after he graduates from college.

Lila's good friend and next-door neighbor Shawn was a very different kind of mother. She partied, smoked marijuana, drank a lot, and roamed the streets at night. She didn't hold a steady job, and she received welfare. Shawn had several live-in boyfriends. She brought in a man who was a crackhead, and another one who lay around on the couch and played video games all day. Shawn supported some of these men along with her son and herself. She put the needs of every man in her life before those of her son. Lila tried to talk to her friend about the way she was raising her son, but Shawn wouldn't listen. She told Lila to mind her own business. When Shawn's son was on his knees gambling on the stoop, she didn't stop him. As a matter of fact, she encouraged him to bring the money home. He dropped out of school and ended up in a jail cell many times throughout his teenage years. Today he is serving a life sentence in prison for armed robbery.

My own parents taught us integrity, even though they were poor people raising children in an impoverished environment. But we always had rules. We had to do our homework when we got home from school. We could not leave our block when we were out playing with our friends. We had to come inside when the streetlights came on outside. We watched TV for an hour or so after dinner and went to bed at nine p.m. Sundays we watched no television. We could only listen to easy listening music on the radio, play board games with each other, or read books. Those Sundays really helped bond us as a family. And I think the rules taught my sisters and brothers and me discipline. I firmly believe they are what children need and want most right now.

Your children can't be more than what you tell them and teach them they can be. In order to teach integrity, you have to have integrity. No matter your circumstances or background, no matter your environment, if you want your children to have a better standard of living, you can make it happen. You just have to want it badly enough. You have to be willing to sacrifice even your own personal comfort and sometimes even your own dreams to make it happen. Lila was determined to write a story for her son's life that differed from her own and the expectations of society. You can encourage reading and mathematics in your home. Turn off the video games and the television. Learn to parent. Despite any odds, you can have a quality of life for yourself and your children that you can be proud of. Just shift your thinking from "I can't" to "I can." If you don't have the personal skills to make this happen, find a role model by looking to someone in your neighborhood, school, or job who you admire and ask for help and direction. As I have said, you *will* have to make sacrifices. (I guarantee you the role model you've chosen has made a lot of them!) I know life is hard for those who are not equipped. But nothing worth having in life is easy. Despite what the television commercial says, there is no "easy button" to push to make things happen. As a parent it is your responsibility to help your child reap a future that is full of hope, opportunity, independence, and all the good things that a parent wants for her child. Ask yourself, what are my intentions for my child's future? Start planting the seeds today. What you provide your children gives them the tools to find their own path to a better life and successful future.

"Life is like a boomerang. Our thoughts, deeds, and words return to us sooner or later, with astounding accuracy."

–GRANT M. BRIGHT

III

AVOID COLLISIONS OF THE HEART: STOP, LISTEN, AND LOOK BOTH WAYS

AUTOBIOGRAPHY IN FIVE SHORT CHAPTERS

I

I walk down the street.
  There is a deep hole in the sidewalk.
  I fall in.
  I am lost . . . . I am helpless.
    It isn't my fault.
It takes forever to find a way out.

II

I walk down the same street.
  There is a deep hole in the sidewalk.
  I pretend I don't see it.
  I fall in again.
I can't believe I am in this same place.
    But, it isn't my fault.
It still takes a long time to get out.

III

I walk down the same street.
  There is a deep hole in the sidewalk.
  I see it is there.
  I still fall in . . . it's a habit . . . but,
    my eyes are open.
    I know where I am.
It is my fault.
I get out immediately.

IV

I walk down the same street.
  There is a deep hole in the sidewalk.
  I walk around it.

V

I walk down another street.

—PORTIA NELSON

Stop Looking for a Man to Validate Who You Are

I often think about how some women project themselves out into the world. I have known very smart, beautiful, and accomplished women who treat themselves as if they are nothing at all.

For instance, I know a forensic odontologist who has been in love with a very handsome man for years. He really doesn't bring much else to the relationship aside from his good looks. She, on the other hand, has published academic papers, completed research studies for major corporations, and amassed an impressive financial portfolio. But she has also done all kinds of humiliating things to keep this man. She's lurked outside of his home to monitor his movements, checked his pockets for other women's phone numbers, and spent hours waiting outside restaurants for dates that he sometimes doesn't show up for. He doesn't even have the decency to call and cancel. She does it all because something about having him on her arm makes her feel complete. This good-looking, underemployed, inconsiderate man makes her feel more important than all of her accomplishments.

And then there's Jane. At one point I was certain that she walked around with a sign on her back that said "beat me," because every man she ever dated physically abused her. Yet each of these men was very wealthy. It was important for her to be able to say, "Oh, Steve is sending a limo to pick me up here for lunch," or "Jamie took me on a shopping spree at Saks Fifth Avenue." She was willing to be reduced to a punching bag because she thought these men with money made her somebody.

You don't need anyone outside of yourself to help you be somebody. This may be difficult to absorb at first, because our culture tells us that we need other people to feel whole. The movies sell us on Cinderella who needs a man to save her. Cinderella was lucky that he happened to be a prince! Every savior won't be. Songs like the one in which Whitney Houston sings "I have nothing, if I don't have you" help perpetuate the concept that women need men to complete their lives. The truth is that people treat you the way you treat yourself. If you don't validate yourself, no person that you let in your heart, home, and bed will validate you either. If you make yourself less so that your partner can feel more important, or if you have to make yourself less so that your partner can make *you* feel more important, then you are giving someone power to put a "validated" stamp on you!

I believe part of the reason that breath is in us is so that we can become a better version of the self with which we came into the world. We simply cannot grow in spirit and wholeness if we give up our power to someone else. If you want to be a powerful person and a powerful attraction in the universe, then you have to know that you are worthy in and of yourself. You are somebody! Realize that that is true whether you are childless, manless, or jobless.

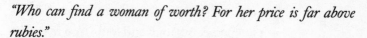

"Who can find a woman of worth? For her price is far above rubies."

–PROVERBS 31:10 (DARBY BIBLE TRANSLATION)

A Fool and Her Money Are Soon Parted

On my television show I have often said: "God protects babies and fools. You're no baby, and the court doesn't protect fools." In one of the cases before me, a woman let a man move into her home after she had known him only a week. He took her body, heart, and four thousand dollars. Another woman lent her brother several thousand dollars knowing he was a gambler. And yet another woman got to know a man on a Christian website and bought him a car before she had even seen him! Listen to me, if you throw gas on a fire in your kitchen, your whole house will burn down. If you do foolish things then the consequences are never going to be positive. It never fails! You just met a man, somebody you barely know, let him move into your house, give him everything he asks for, and you think he's going to treat you like a queen? It's not going to happen. You can't go crying, "Oh, why does he treat me this way?" You let him in; he didn't force his way into your house at gunpoint. You showered him with gifts and goodies and he treated you like a doormat. But YOU let him in! So you gotta learn to own the responsibility for your actions as well as the consequences of your actions. You are responsible for respecting yourself and behaving in ways that create respect from the men you come into contact with.

A woman, Christina, who I once represented, pinned her hopes for more than twenty years on gaining the love of the same man. They met when she was barely out of her teens, and he eventually fathered three of her children. The third child was conceived after the man had moved on and married another woman. Christina and the new Mrs. were pregnant at the same time! That the man had moved on to another woman and to another family did not stop and has not stopped Christina from continually making a fool of herself. She has bought him airline tickets and financed vacations that included members of his new family in order to remain close to him. She has run up her credit cards by buying him expensive clothes, electronic gadgets, and gourmet restaurant dinners. Now mind you, he is married and has a whole other family. But Christina is willing to accept the crumbs of time and affection that he doles out to her as he pleases. She hasn't gotten smart enough to realize that he only comes around when he needs something.

You know what the saddest part of Christina's situation

is? It's the message that she is sending to her children. She is giving her children a warped message about the way male and female relationships work. She has set a horrible example for them about dignity and worth. Trying to help her see her foolish ways is like talking to a brick wall. The double-timing man lost his job in the recession, so Christina borrowed money against her credit cards so that he could pay to keep his other family above water. At last report Christina is totally maxed out on her credit cards, in danger of foreclosure on her mortgage, and still hasn't figured out that she is playing the part of a fool. Christina, and the other women in these stories, have diverted their aspirations and goals to someone outside of themselves. They have all turned the wheel over to someone else. They may have paid for the trip, but they are not driving!

How can you ever learn to stay in your lane if you have turned over the operation and direction of your life to someone else? It reminds me of a car commercial that says: "On the road of life, there are passengers and there are drivers." Which are you? If someone else is at your wheel, then you are a passenger and you should be the one in control of where you're heading.

A fool doesn't have to remain a fool forever. If you see yourself behaving in the ways I've talked about, it may mean you are lacking in self-worth. Loving yourself is a growing process, but to get any flower to grow, you have to eliminate the weeds that may be choking it. You can grow into your full bloom. I want to help you get there. But we have to get rid of those weeds! Admitting your foolish ways is the first step in any recovery. You know how an alcoholic stands up in those meetings and says my name is so and so and I'm an alcoholic? That's right, you too, Missy, need to get in front of that mirror and profess the truth—you are a fool and you want to change your foolish ways. This is important because if you can't be truthful to yourself, when absolutely nobody else is around to experience your naked truth, then you'll never be able to change and you'll never be the best you can be. The act of being truthful and calling out your foolishness allows you to name it and claim it. And once you have claimed it, you will be able to look at your situation and your future with new eyes. Love, when it's real and good and true, never comes with a price tag. If you are bidding on love with money, sex, or trinkets, then you always run the risk of losing out to a higher bidder. But rest assured, it's not all gloom and doom. You can recover, and I strongly urge you to do so real fast. Otherwise, get a second job and a pen that works because you'll be writing a lot of checks.

⊢—

"What the superior person seeks is in himself; what the small person seeks is in others."

—CONFUCIUS

You Are Not a Punching Bag

When I was elected to the bench in 2000, I was required to attend Judges' College along with all the other newly elected judges around the state of Florida. The two-week intensive session had workshops on every matter important to being a good judge. We learned everything from the mechanics of issuing proper arrest warrants to developing cultural sensitivity on the bench.

During a break between sessions, I was sitting outside getting some sun. We were in Tallahassee in January, and it was frigid cold outside, but the sun was shining and the azaleas were about to bloom. I was soaking up the sun and the scenery when I saw this thirty-something woman being pushed in a wheelchair into the conference room where the next session was about to begin. I opened my notebook to look at the day's schedule and read the words "special speaker." Up to that point, all of the sessions had been conducted by senior judges or legal experts, so I was curious about who this young woman might be.

When we all reconvened in the conference room, this woman was up on the stage sitting in front of the microphone. Her name was Martha, and she told us that she was from a prominent family in central Florida. Her father had been the owner of a local Ford dealership, and she had driven a brand-new car every year since she was a teenager. When she went off to college, she met the man who would become her husband. She told us that he had always had a jealous streak from early on in their relationship. At first, she believed that he wanted to spend all of his time with her and questioned her whereabouts because he loved her so much. She wasn't the only woman who ever thought love is about possessiveness. I believed it too at one time. Others believe it still.

Once Martha graduated from college, she got a job as a probation officer. Matters got worse with her husband. He grew jealous of her time spent at work. He began drinking and calling her horrible names. Eventually the abuse became physical and her husband was beating her daily. Martha's husband was arrested for domestic violence and ordered to stay away from her. He continued to contact her by telephone, despite the court order. He would cry and beg her to come back to him, promising her that he would change. She would spot him following her around town.

She never reported these communications or actions to the court, even though he was in violation of the restraining order. She did not take him back though! Smart woman! She filed for divorce and set about the business of picking up the pieces and moving on. One day as she got out of her car, her husband came running out from behind some bushes toward her with a gun. She ran, and he shot her four times. As she lay on the sidewalk looking up at him, her husband pointed the gun toward her head and fired another shot. That shot missed and hit the pavement. He then raised his gun to his head and, as Martha watched, fired his last shot into his temple, killing himself.

Martha told us that during rehabilitation she started thinking about domestic violence. She was now paralyzed with only the use of her right arm. She wondered how she had missed the warning signs and how she could help the courts, the police, and other women in her situation. She now spends her time speaking to judges and police departments and offering support to victims of domestic violence. She said that she is very happy to be alive and that God spared her for a reason. When she speaks to domestic violence victims, she tells them: "Take control of your life now. Look at me. But don't think of me as a victim, think of me as a survivor." I have never forgotten her story and remember it every time I have to deal with women struggling to escape violence in their own homes.

One day I was shopping in Walgreens. A young woman came up behind me and asked, "Are you Judge Francis?" I said I was, and she asked if I remembered her. She reminded me of the facts surrounding her domestic violence case in my courtroom. She had been involved with a boy who treated her as his personal punching bag. Once when she had gotten the courage to leave him, she packed her bags and walked with her things to the bus stop. He saw her standing on the corner as he was coming home. He pulled his car into the yard, got out, and ran to the bus stop. He grabbed her by her hair and dragged her kicking and screaming all the way back to the house and proceeded to beat her until her face was swollen. The next morning, she called her father, who picked her up and took her directly to the courthouse to apply for a restraining order. In Florida, temporary restraining orders are issued on the sworn testimony of the person seeking the restraining order. If the judge believes that sufficient facts exist for the issuance of such an order, then she issues it temporarily for fifteen days. The sheriff then serves the offending party, and a hearing is set on the fifteenth day so the court can have a full hearing where both parties will be heard. Many women lose the nerve to come to court after they get a temporary order, so the court ends up dismissing the case entirely at the permanent hearing. But this particular young woman came to court before me at the hearing on the permanent order. She told me that she did not want to pursue a permanent order. The boyfriend stood silently at the defense podium.

Something about his demeanor and the way she spoke told me she was terrified of him. I asked her if she realized that if I dismissed the case, she would have no order of protection against this man, and that he would be free to call, text, email, and show up at her door. She said she wasn't afraid of him and wanted the case dismissed. On a hunch, I told the boyfriend to have a seat *inside* the courtroom and told the woman to go *outside* and really think about whether she would feel safe without the order. I told her I would re-call her case at the end of the calendar. For the rest of the calendar, the boyfriend remained inside the courtroom, and I had my bailiff take his cell phone. At the end of the calen-dar, I recalled the case. The woman said she wanted to go forward. I asked the boyfriend if he had testimony to offer or if he had an objection to the permanent order. He said: "She can have it. I got another woman already." I signed an order restraining him from having any contact with her either di-rectly or through friends and family members.

So now here she was standing behind me at Walgreens. She said she was a manager there. She wanted to thank me for giving her the time outside the courtroom to think about that order. She was glad she had gone forward. Shortly after I issued the order, the boyfriend showed up at the house where the woman was living with her father. It was two o'clock in the morning, and he tried to break in through the front door. Her father shot and killed him.

I share these stories to give you an idea about the look and feel of domestic violence. Many people have in their minds that it affects only people of certain ethnic or eco-nomic backgrounds. It can affect anybody. I have had my own experience with it and learned to recognize the signs of a potential abuser a mile away. Staying in your lane is about doing what you must to take control of the wheel of your life. Make no excuses. Be smart, not a statistic. Heed the warning signs ahead. Anyone who is possessive, degrading, or alienating you from family and friends is abusing you. Period.

—

"No one can make you feel inferior without your consent."
–ELEANOR ROOSEVELT

Your Son Is Not Your Man

While sitting on the bench in criminal court, I came across many disadvantaged young men who were clueless about manhood and all the responsibilities that come with it. Case after case, conviction after conviction, these "boys" were clueless about what they were doing, the path they were taking in life, and how to have personal accountability. At the beginning of my career I would often ask "What in the world is going on here"? While I held each of these boys 100 percent responsible for the crimes they committed, I came to realize that in most cases there was an "unaccountable" accomplice in crime. It was their mothers! The truth of the matter is, there are increasing numbers of single-parent households in which mothers have developed unhealthy, nonparental relationships with their sons, who are looked at and treated as if they were the mother's boyfriend or husband and referred to as "the man of the house." This is a very disturbing and unhealthy trend. It is also one that has enormous implications not only for the mother and her son, but for our society as a whole.

In private practice, I represented a defendant, Tyrone, charged with drug trafficking. He was a high school dropout about nineteen years old. The first time he came to my office he came with his mother. Every time I asked Tyrone a question, his mother answered it. It got to the point that I flippantly asked her: "Were you out there on the street selling drugs with your son? Will you let him answer?" And she said: "He's shy. He's slow. He's not comfortable." As I continued recounting the litany of Tyrone's prior drug charges, she made excuses for him ranging from "He was hanging with a bad crowd" to "The police set him up." She had succeeded in emasculating this young man. She discouraged his relationships with girls and supported his decision to drop out of school in eleventh grade. She hadn't taught him discipline, had no expectations for him, and gave him no responsibilities while growing up. By supporting his weakness, she created a person who was totally dependent on her.

Tyrone's mother had three daughters, and he was her only son. In the black community we often say that a mother raises her daughters but loves her sons. Girls are raised to be more responsible than boys. Girls are taught to clean house, wash clothes, take care of their younger siblings, and so forth. The expectations for sons are very different. Tyrone's mother catered to him like a king. And like a king, he was never wrong, never at fault. She professed his innocence in every criminal case he ever had. But this time the prosecutor had video surveillance of the corner where Tyrone was selling drugs. There was footage of him doing hand-to-hand drug transactions, and when the police went in to grab him they found a stash of drugs behind him. His fingerprints were all over the baggies that contained the cocaine. The state offered him a "sweetheart" deal of five years if he pled guilty. I say sweetheart because that penalty was a lot less severe than the fifteen-year minimum mandatory he faced if a jury convicted him.

Since he had been caught red-handed, I advised him that it would be in his best interest to accept the deal. As I explained the plea offer to Tyrone, his mother said: "I can't live without my baby for five years in jail. Ms. Mills, he didn't do it. I don't care what the police say; it's a setup." I said: "Ma'am, Tyrone is a grown man. And he is my client. Why don't you wait outside while he and I discuss his case?" She left in a huff but not before warning: "He's not going to make a decision without me, just you wait and see. You'll be calling me right back in here." I tried talking to Tyrone and all I could pry out of him were simple yeses or nos. Look what this loving momma had created! I realized I wasn't getting anything out of this boy. Momma was his mouthpiece. Finally I laid it out for him, "Tyrone, you can take the five years or risk the fifteen." All he said was, "I have to talk it over with my momma."

Tyrone went to trial because his momma couldn't live

without her man for five years. He was found guilty after the jury deliberated only long enough to eat lunch. As the judge sentenced Tyrone to the minimum fifteen years, I heard a loud wailing in the back of the courtroom. I whipped around and saw Tyrone's mother pop up from her seat and start ripping her clothes off, stripping them off layer by layer until she was completely naked, and then run out of the courtroom. She sprinted up and down the hallway, crying, "Jesus! They took my baby away! Oh, my God!" She was taken away in restraints to a nearby psychiatric facility.

Tyrone's story is not uncommon. Now, before any of you decide to bombard my Facebook page with a bunch of colorful messages, you should know that I do realize that there are plenty of strong, single women who are doing a fine job raising their sons. My personal assistant is a single mother who has done a FABULOUS job raising her college-bound son. However, I don't see them in the courtroom (and I'm very happy to say that). The ones I *do* see are the statistics that are reported daily on the news. This is really complicated, folks, because truthfully, it's not about the sons. It has more to do with the mothers and their histories and relationships with men. A woman who has been mistreated by a man, or who has loved a man who never returned her love, may be working out her "stuff" through her son. These women tend to relax the rules with their sons because then, maybe, they figure, they'll love them back, unconditionally, and for always; or these mothers become indispensable to their sons because then, maybe, their sons will always need and want them in their lives; or these mothers become their sons' number-one "girl" because then, maybe, even when they have a wife or girlfriend she'll still always remain their number-one girl. Isn't this what women do with their men? Let's be honest.

Oftentimes, when men tell us who they are, we attempt to change them into who we want them to be. In an attempt to make herself feel loved and validated, this type of mother prevents any possibility of her son becoming an independent, self-thinking man. Although it is not her intention, it is most definitely the end result, and everyone pays for it. She pays every time he commits a crime and has to do time in jail, all because he was raised without boundaries and was made to think that he walked on water; he pays every time he fails to understand that there are real consequences to his actions and ends up losing precious years from his life because he never learned or was not taught the lesson; and society pays because he's either hurting us through violence, costing us through taxes, and/or cheating us of his potential brilliance and contribution to society.

Momma, you have to stop loving your son to failure and start raising him to success. Encourage your son to enroll in classes in his school that are taught by positive male figures. Signing your son up for sports either at school or in the community is also a good way to develop confidence and pride, which are two key ingredients for success. There are resources that can help you if there is no active father or father figure in your child's life. Organizations such as 100 Black Men, Big Brothers, Concerned Black Men (CBM), Boys to Men, and more will help partner your son with mentors who are leaders, businessmen, coaches, and other professionals who are positive role models in your particular community. I urge you to contact one or all of these organizations for help. You owe it to yourself and, most important, you owe it to the son you're raising.

"A mother is not a person to lean on, but a person to make leaning unnecessary."

–Dorothy Canfield Fisher

Is Your Small Talk Small?

A couple of years ago I was invited to be the guest speaker at a luncheon in Chicago that was part of a week-long women's summit sponsored by a local radio station. Instead of giving a speech, I decided it would be fun to sit down and have a rap session with the women and talk about some of the things that were going on in their lives. For two hours we talked about subjects ranging from child rearing to dealing with problem neighbors to shopping for bargains. Eventually, the conversation got around to dating and relationships. Whenever I have this type of interaction with women, the topic of men always finds its way into the conversation. In the Chicago group, there were women in long-term committed relationships, but the majority of the women were single.

As the discussion progressed, I started to hear the senti-
ment that I hear over and over again from women, which is
that many of them are dissatisfied with the choices for male
companionship available out there. If I haven't heard it a
thousand times, I haven't heard it once: "It's hard to find a
good man." I know this to be true from my own experiences. As I have gotten older and more financially independent, it has become more challenging to meet single men
on the same page. And I also have friends who are accomplished and successful who bemoan the lack of available
singles to date. The reality is that women outnumber men
three to one in America, and you have to discount in that
statistic the men who are gay, married, incarcerated, will-
fully unemployed, and mentally ill. So the prospects are limited statistically *and* realistically. In my own life, I find that
men show up on my path when I am not even thinking
about a relationship. As a matter of fact, the more I focus on
creating my best life and pursuing my own interests, the
more I seem to attract male interest. It's sort of like watching the phone and waiting for it to ring. When you take
your attention off the phone and start putting away the
dishes or cleaning out the closet that you have put off
straightening for months, then suddenly the phone begins
ringing off the hook. The same thing is true in life. Once
you stop searching for a man and start searching for yourself and focusing on your dreams, men start showing up out
of the woodwork. And sometimes Mr. "Right For You"
shows up too. It's true!

I think if you want to attract a quality man, you have to

be a quality attraction yourself. I am not talking about on-the-surface attractiveness. That is important too. But the more important question is: How do you look on the inside? I have met hundreds of women like the women in Chicago. What many have in common is a laundry list of the qualities that they are looking for in a man. They want someone who is tall, handsome, sensitive, hardworking, successful, financially secure, funny, compassionate, and romantic, and who is also an attentive and accomplished lover. When women tell me what they want in a man, I ask them, "And what do you bring to the table?" Some women can come up with only a short list in comparison to the long list they carry around in their mind to compare against the men they date. I don't know your particular circumstances, but I do know that the more interesting a person is, male or female, the more attractive they are to the opposite sex. So, if you want to meet interesting people, you have to be interesting yourself. If you want to have healthy relationships, you have to be healthy yourself.

Have you ever been around a person who is desperate? Did you sense the desperation in the person's voice or actions? Well, other people, including men, can smell your desperation a mile away. And desperate people are vulnerable and easy to take advantage of. So stop being desperate to find happiness outside yourself and start to focus on creating your best life for a while and watch what happens. Read and learn more, explore your world, expand your mind more, and lose yourself in the life you are in the process of creating. You will not only enrich your own life, you will also be creating a magnet of attraction called "you." Does a magnet have to go around looking for metal to attach itself to, or does all the metal attach to the magnet whenever the magnet is near?

Think of your life as a novel that you are in the process of writing. You are the heroine in your novel. Is she someone you can't stop reading about page after page, or can you sum up who she is in a page or two? Or worse, is she someone who complains about the people and circumstances of her life to all her friends and family who will listen? Nothing appealing about that either. I know women who go out on dates and spend the entire time telling the new man about all the horrible men they have dated in the past. What's that about? If you met a man who dogged and put down women during his first date with you, you would run like heck to get away from him. Maybe you're pushing people away by the negativity or narrow-mindedness of your conversation without even knowing it. Have you heard the saying, "Small minds discuss people, average minds discuss things, but great minds discuss ideas?" If you start to explore life's treasures for growth and fulfillment, you will be able to elevate your conversation game too. You will begin to notice, almost immediately, that when you are focusing on creating your best life, good things and good people will start appearing in it. Enthusiasm is contagious. When you are living the life you love, your enthusiasm, not your desperation, will shine through. Then the road ahead will open up with a world of new people and new opportunities. In expanding your mind, you have to consider that love may not come in a package that looks like you either. Are you limiting yourself to men of a certain race, nationality, or age group? If so, you are doing yourself a disservice and should consider other avenues of available men. I do!

I am not writing this to tell you to transform yourself any one way or another in the pursuit of a relationship. And I am not telling you that if you are the most outgoing, wonderful woman in the world that you are going to meet your prince charming. But I am telling you that your only around-the-clock pursuit should be the one that takes you further in self-discovery and personal fulfillment. Staying in your lane is about taking care of your business to create the best "you" possible. And when you take your view off the pursuit of a man and turn your eyes back to your own pursuits for your personal bests, only God knows what miracles are waiting for you just around the bend! Just keep driving.

▐━

"It is more important to know where you are going than to get there quickly. Don't mistake activity for achievement."
–MABEL NEWCOMBER

IV

ROAD WORK AHEAD — RECONSTRUCTING YOU

Nobody Likes a Pest, Which Is Why We Have Pesticide

I believe there are three deadly social sins: calling your friends and family constantly (even though they aren't returning the calls); showing up at the homes of friends and acquaintances without invitation or prior announcement; and not realizing that the party is over. These behaviors are disrespectful to the people on the receiving end of the thoughtlessness, and amount to pestering. The behavior will not stop until the underlying problem is dealt with: finding a fulfilling life for yourself and not looking for others to create it for you.

When I was in my twenties, taking a two-year break between college and law school, a distant relative of mine, Myrna, started calling me constantly and popping up at my home unexpectedly. Once there, she never knew when to go home. We had never been that close, but she had heard that I was taking time off before law school and made it her business to keep me company, whether I needed it or not. This was before caller ID, so there were times when I was afraid to answer the phone because I feared that it would be Myrna hounding me. And the conversation was always mundane; she didn't speak about anything of real consequence. She kept reliving her high school years in every conversation we had, and she'd graduated ten years earlier! Being a cheerleader and homecoming queen had been the highlight of her life. Do you know anybody like that? One day, she came by and I didn't answer the door. My family had a patio set outside, and she sat out there waiting for me to come home. My car was parked in the yard, so she must've figured I'd be back home shortly. Eventually I felt small as a bug and wound up letting her in, making up an excuse about being in the shower or something to explain why I did not hear the bell.

One day I thought, "This is ridiculous, and I shouldn't have to play hide-and-seek in my own home." I finally told Myrna that she was calling and coming by too much. I asked her what was she doing with her life. She replied that other than her job, she didn't have much else to do. She did nothing for fun, she didn't have any real relationships, and she was living in the past. No wonder she was constantly pestering me! I told her, "You need to get an adult life because the teenage memories that you are living on are of no importance now, and dwelling on them is preventing you from having a full life." That afternoon we talked and delved deep to the root of the problem. And the problem was that Myrna felt that her life had come to a dead standstill and didn't look like it was moving anywhere soon. I urged her to start thinking about all the childhood dreams she had had about what she wanted her adult life to look like. Myrna began to search for a deeper meaning for her life. Then one day she announced that she had discovered Buddhism. A coworker invited her to a chanting session, and it turned Myrna on to a whole new spiritual path to fulfillment. She became busy because she was chanting two or three times a week with this group. She developed new interests and friendships, and rarely had the time to call. She didn't even have the time to return MY phone calls!

Last I heard, she was teaching English to Muslim children in Africa. Teaching in a foreign country had been something she had dreamed of doing ever since her childhood. But you know, something else came out of that situation for me. I had an epiphany. Sometimes God puts people in front of us as mirrors. I started thinking about my own life after my talk with Myrna. I had been out of college for nearly two years, always telling folks that I was going to law school. I started to wonder if Myrna had chosen the friendship with me because she saw me as some sort of kindred spirit. Had my life become pointless too? What was I really doing? I had to admit to myself that, just like Myrna, I too had become stuck and stopped growing. It was as though I had pulled over to a rest stop and set up camp. I was no longer on the road heading toward my lifelong dream of being a trial lawyer. I was telling Myrna to get back out there on her journey, and I myself was in a rut! Hmmm, practice what you preach?

So ask yourself, do you have to make three phone calls to someone for every one call returned? Do you show up at people's houses unannounced and the doorbell goes unanswered even though there are cars in the driveway and the lights are on in the living room? Are the last of the partygoers saying good night to the hostess at the front door as you are pouring your next drink? Then it may be time to take a look at your life.

Some of this may be because you feel lonely, which we all feel from time to time. But our loneliness is not someone else's problem; it's our own issue. We need to learn to deal with it, like Myrna, and question why it's there. If you want friends, you must be a friend, and friends are respectful of each other's time, space, and privacy. Think about your dreams. Start taking classes, going to book readings, museums, the circus, whatever it is that interests you. When you start filling in your own gaps, you will start to cherish your own time, space, and privacy. Not only will your life be richer, friendships will be too!

▬▬

"The rung of a ladder was never meant to rest upon, but only to hold a man's foot long enough to enable him to put the other somewhat higher."
—THOMAS HENRY HUXLEY

Are You a Busybody?

Most folks who didn't grow up in Florida really don't think of Miami as the South, but I can assure you that the Miami I grew up in was as southern as any city south of the Mason-Dixon line. At least in the black neighborhoods. My great-grandmother raised chickens in her yard. Kids were taught to answer "yes, ma'am," and "no, ma'am" when addressing adult women. We called our undergarments petticoats long after the rest of the country called them slips.

I grew up in an apartment building with four one-bedroom units that was across the street from a juke joint called The Screened Inn, where every weekend there was a lot of partying and drinking. And occasionally fights. In our building there was a little garden shaded by an avocado tree. Sister Dozier, Miss Sis, and Miss Alberta were women in the building who would gather in the late afternoon under this tree, sitting in chairs in a circle. They would bring out collard greens to clean, pole beans to snap, and potatoes to peel. Miss Alberta and Miss Sis dipped snuff. Now, snuff is a moist type of tobacco you place between your lips and gums, and you get the benefits of tobacco without having to actually smoke it. The user has to periodically spit out thick brown wads of the stuff. Let me tell you, it's not a pretty sight (not ladylike at all), and you certainly wouldn't forget it if you ever saw it done. Anyway, they sat around in the front yard in their aprons preparing their vegetables for the evening meal, sternly shooing away us kids: "Go play! And stop looking in grown folks' mouths!"

I loved to listen in on their conversations anyway. They talked about all kinds of stuff in between spitting out tobacco. But some way or other the conversation always gravitated back to the fast women who hung out at The Screened Inn. The garden women used words like "fresh" and "fast tail" and "loose" to describe them. On Friday evenings, when the joint across the road was really jumping, invariably, one of these "fresh" women could be spotted tumbling out of the inn on the arm of a man whose paycheck was burning a hole in his pocket. When the garden ladies saw this sort of action, they would say, "Oh, she is ready to get busy!" You know what they meant. From my child's vantage point, I saw that nothing good could come of these "busy bodies." Their lives seemed to be complicated by the babies they couldn't or wouldn't take care of (some of their kids went to my school), ill treatment by men, and the contempt from women who were trying to create a safe and healthy home for their own children. No self-respecting woman would be seen in the company of this type of woman.

Years later, when I first heard the Luther Vandross song "Busybody," it immediately took me back to those "fresh" women at The Screened Inn. He croons, "You're a busy-body, giving all of your love to just anybody. You never say no, you never say no." "Busybody," for me, meant a woman who sleeps around carelessly with different people, some-times for financial gain, has children who have no real su-pervision and guidance, and who is simply traveling a destructive path to nowhere. Are you one of these women? Remember, all whores aren't streetwalkers, you know? Sleeping around not only compromises your mental, spiri-tual, and physical health, but also affects your public image. Your reputation can be more powerful than your presence and often precedes you. It is hard to navigate the road of life by avoiding toll roads. You have to pay your own way on your journey. Hopping from bed to bed is just a shortcut to a dead end. Integrity and reputation go hand in hand. They are often the stongest foundation that we can stand on. It is hard to get back up on that platform when its strength has been compromised by your poor behavior and lack of judg-ment.

When I was a public defender in Miami, my secretary briefed me on a new client. Her name was Angelita, and she was charged with more than fifty separate counts of shoplifting. Angelita was a tall woman with mocha skin and large, swaying hips. The first day I met her, she came in swinging those hips and smacking gum, and accompanying her was a nondescript man who she said was her boyfriend, who said nothing during our entire interview. I eventually filed a motion to consolidate all of her shoplifting cases so they would be brought to one judge's division and be resolved all at once. Over the course of many months I gathered information and questioned various witnesses for the cases. Angelita and I had several meetings, and every time she came in to see me she was with a different man! She always introduced him as "my boyfriend." One day I asked her: "You're doing all of this stealing, yet you have all of these different 'boyfriends.' Are they doing anything for you?" She said: "I handle my business, Ms. Mills. You just handle my case and don't worry about me." I was thinking: You can't be handling your business too well. These are just the cases where they actually caught you shoplifting. Who knows how many times you got away with it?

The last time I saw her she was a shadow of her former self. Her once-beautiful skin now hung from her shrunken frame. She was sweating, and kept wiping her forehead with a rag she pulled out of her purse. This time she came alone. She told me she had a virus, and she wasn't exactly sure what it was, but she was sick. Immediately, the letters HIV popped into my head. She exhibited the visible symptoms the media warned people about back then in the infancy of AIDS. She said she didn't know exactly what was wrong with her, but she wouldn't be able to make it to the hearing we'd set for her case. She said it took everything to drag herself down to my office. I asked her about the many men who had accompanied her over the past few months. Couldn't one of them drive her to court so she could get this criminal case off of her plate? Angelita said she didn't have anybody, and besides, now she needed to worry about her health.

I got her case reset a couple of times but eventually the judge got fed up with the absences. He said she had to come in; otherwise he was issuing a warrant for her arrest. This was in the 1980s at the very beginning of the AIDS epidemic, so the court wasn't sensitive to these issues yet. A woman who identified herself as Angelita's aunt called to tell me that my client had been hospitalized and wasn't well enough to come to the mandatory hearings. Her aunt went on to say that she didn't know what she was going to do with Angelita's children. I was shocked. I never knew she had kids! Her aunt told me she had eight. And she was thirty years old. At the next hearing, I brought a letter from the hospital stating her condition, and her aunt also came in to testify that Angelita was very ill. The aunt came into court with this troupe of eight children. As they stood in front of the court, they were like stair steps ascending in height, as if Angelita had them once a year, and they barely looked related to one another. All I could think of was that this woman had led this life of crime, obviously sleeping around with many different men, and now her poor choices were going to leave these children motherless. But the other thing that struck me that day in court was how dirty and malnourished her children were. During a break in the proceedings, I made a call to Children and Family Services to make an anonymous report of suspected child neglect and abuse. This eventually led to an inspector going to the home and schools of these kids to assess their living environment. All of those kids were placed in foster care. I learned that Angelita had a long history with the agency. In fact, the children had all been in and out of foster care. Once a child was taken from her at the hospital soon after delivery. It was born addicted to cocaine.

Angelita died a week after the hearing. Who knows how she contracted HIV, but I'm sure the revolving door of different men didn't help. I feel that it's important for me to let you know my views and sensibilities toward HIV. I have friends who are HIV positive, and one of my best friends passed away twelve years ago from this most dreaded disease. My friend's passing was one of the most painful times of my life. HIV knows no color, sex, age, or sexual orientation. You can be in a committed relationship, heterosexual or homosexual, in which your partner may have slept with someone else who was infected. It only takes one time. The two groups that are currently experiencing the highest rate of HIV infection in the United States are teenagers and heterosexual women, mainly women of color. We have to take responsibility for the things that we can control, and one thing we have absolute control over is decisions about our own bodies. We must take every precaution to protect them.

The cruelest dagger to a woman's reputation is being labeled or treated as a whore. She will never gain the respect of men or women by being one. Being a busybody means you have taken your eyes off living a full and joyful life in exchange for moments of "present pleasure." Check your dress, your talk, your walk, and the number of "baby daddy"s you have to take to court. There are a lot of things you may want to be in life, but being a busybody leads down a low road, and we are striving for the high road.

"Watch your thoughts, for they become words. Watch your words, for they become actions. Watch your actions, for they become habits. Watch your habits, for they become character. Watch your character, for it becomes your destiny."

—UNKNOWN

What Have You Learned from Your Garden?

I've learned a lot about life from plants. I have
learned what works to sustain life, and what
amounts to neglect. I have also learned that
the same care and maintenance you provide one
type of plant could actually kill another. I feel closest to God and the spiritual world when I am tending to my plants. Even when I had no house or
yard, I kept container gardens on my apartment
balcony.

I think my love of flowers and plants comes from
my grandfather Lee, who had an orchid plant someone had given him in the 1970s, which grew huge,
beautiful lavender flowers. When I was elected as a
judge, my grandfather was too ill to come to my in-
vestiture. He sent me three lovely blooms from the
orchid. Those orchids represented a part of himself

that he was sharing with me. When he passed away a few years later, I asked my grandmother if we could split the plant. It was more than thirty years old, but Granddaddy had nurtured it so that it continued to bloom. I never grew orchids before, so I did everything for her (to me, all orchids are women). I fed it charcoal, orchid food, and potting mulch, and I hung the plant under the shade of a tree similar to the one in my grandparents' yard. After several months went by without the orchid blooming, I went to see Mr. Lester, a very old and wise southerner from Mississippi who owns a nursery. I have sought his advice on plants for many years. He told me: "Sometimes after you've created the 'home' for a plant to grow, you just have to let go . . . ignore it for a while. Ignoring it is not a bad thing once you have given a plant all that it needs. You've done enough; you are overnurturing her. Just leave it alone."

When I was married, my husband and I owned a home that had azaleas growing beneath several oak trees. As a rule, azaleas do not generally grow in subtropical areas like Miami, so every time a gardener or sprinkler repairman came into my yard, they'd be shocked to see the plants. They would say "Are those azaleas?! In Miami?" I started reading up on azaleas when we first bought the house and ordered fertilizers from companies as far away as Seattle and New Orleans, all to get them to blossom. I pruned them and gave them artificial light; I did everything to make them deliver their beautiful pink flowers. My husband and I were always working on these azaleas, doing everything for them.

In 1999 my husband died, and I went on a journey as a part of my grief process. I left my house and my family and drove through the Carolinas, Virginia, and Washington, D.C., where my best friend lives and who was my "rock" during that sad period in my life. After a month or so, I flew back home to Miami and took a taxi home from the airport. As the cab driver pulled into my yard, I saw that all the azaleas were in full bloom! It was as if they all were saying, "Hello, welcome home. We've missed you!" I started to cry uncontrollably in the backseat of the cab. For five or six years we'd been working on those azaleas, and they had *never...ever* flowered.

How plants grow correlates with life's growth process. You do all that you can, you throw your best into something, and then you have to step back and just let it happen. When you know that you've done your best, there is nothing more that you can do except wait. Be patient. Let it unfold. I find that that is the difficult part. We are so "now" oriented that we have grown out of tune with the natural cycle of things, but we need to allow the universe *its* time to work things out. It's not on our time, it's on God's time. Simple advice, but too often not heeded.

I have tried to exercise patience for the process of growth in my own life. When I was shopping around for a house ten years ago I looked at more than fifty houses. I'm sure I drove my realtor crazy because I always found something lacking in the houses he showed me. I prayed to God to help me find the house of my dreams at a price I could afford. One day, traffic was diverted from my normal route to work, and I found myself waiting behind a line of cars on a street that I had never been on before. As I looked over, I saw this house. I was in love with it though it was not for sale. Even though I had no idea what the house looked like on the inside, I knew it was the house I had been looking for. I asked my realtor if he could contact the owner to see if he had any interest in selling it. The realtor said he had never done such a thing, but he agreed to find out who the owner was and contact him. When the realtor called the owner, the owner told him that he was in love with his house and had absolutely no intention of ever selling it. With this news, I declared that I was through with searching for a house because I had found my dream house and it wasn't available. Six months later, the owner of the house contacted my realtor to ask if I was still interested in buying his house because he and his wife were divorcing. I bought the house. God had delivered my dream house to me according to His timetable. I just had to to be patient. By the way, Granddaddy's orchid? Just when I had almost forgotten about her, I came home one day and a flash of lavender caught the corner of my eye in the garden. She had presented to me three beautiful blooms! In her own time.

So what have *you* learned from your garden?

⊢

"Earth and sky, woods and fields, lakes and rivers, the mountains and the sea, are excellent schoolmasters and teach us more than books."

–JOHN LUBBOCK

Life Isn't Always Black and White

When I was in central Florida working on this book with my niece, we had this idea that we were going to walk on the beach every day and clear our heads, exchange ideas, and get in shape. On the third or fourth day of walking on the beach, I saw that we had ended up near an apartment building where I'd stayed a few years earlier. It was a beautiful, century-old building on some land behind a gated community of high-end homes. I wanted my niece to see the place for its beauty and grand architecture. A guard came out of his station as we approached the gate, and I asked him if the place I was looking for was behind the gate. He said, "This is an exclusive community. Are you two looking for work?" His words stopped me dead in my tracks! I looked him straight in the eye without missing a beat and asked, "Do I *look* like I'm looking for work here?" He stammered out a no.

His problem was that he really didn't look at us. He saw us, but he did not look at us. What he saw were two black women dressed casually with covered hair, and he assumed we were looking for housekeeping jobs. We could not possibly have any business behind the gate otherwise.

Being a good judge means looking beyond culture, color, age, and dress. Too often people act and judge based on an immediate perception of what's in front of us. I believe in order to grow, and be happy, healthy and well-rounded, a person has to develop cultural, social, and economic sensitivity to people. It helps us to not fall into the trap of judging or categorizing people by preconceived notions. I had a dear and close friend, Rodney, who died several years ago who used to say, "Once you label me, you negate me." Once you call me short, Jewish, gay, old, a southerner, religious, etc., you have placed limits on all the other things I can be and you will interact with me based on the label you have given me. We might as well go around with blinders on and not have a brain if we are going to judge a person and put him in a category. And it was offensive to me and I'm sure it was offensive to my niece that this man automatically thought we were there looking for jobs as housekeepers. Of course, I have nothing but respect for housekeepers. I have one, and I respect her enormously as a person first and secondly as an individual who takes great pride in her work. I have cleaned other people's toilets my-self. But that's not the point here.

You might think that maybe this happened because we were dressed in casual clothes, but time and time again I have met up with the very same narrow mind-set while shopping in stores from the likes of TJ Maxx to Saks Fifth Avenue. It makes no difference. I have been dressed in high heels and panty hose, holding a vintage handbag, with my hair and makeup done, and invariably a customer will come up to me and ask, "Do you work here?" I stop, making sure to look them straight in the eye as I ask in return, "Do I *look* like I work here?" The person, usually a woman, will an-swer, "No, you don't," a bit shamefacedly. It's because they are not looking *at me*. We need to start looking people in the eye and assessing them. I would have had a better experi-ence with the guard at the gate (and I assure you he would've had a better experience with me) if he had just looked at me as a person first. Remember, others are travel-ing alongside you who may not look, act, or think like you. Staying in your lane means respecting other people's differ-ences as well as their right to travel the road too.

"When you judge another, you do not define them, you define yourself."
—DR. WAYNE DYER

Don't Dream It, Be It!

When I was an undergraduate at Bowdoin College in Brunswick, Maine, there was a two-hundred-year-old house on campus named the John Brown Russwurm Afro-American Center. John Brown Russwurm became the first African American to graduate from Bowdoin and the second to graduate from an American college. Although Russwurm was a student at the university, he wasn't allowed to live with the other students. He had to work in the kitchen, and he couldn't join the fraternities and campus clubs. He was treated like a second-class citizen because of his skin color.

Beginning in 1970, the college allowed two African American students to stay in the John Brown Russwurm house, and during my sophomore year, I had the honor of living there. There were living quarters upstairs, and the Afro-American studies department was downstairs. A few times a week I would stop by the department to shoot the breeze with Tammy, the secretary. She was married to a domineering day laborer with whom she had three very young children. She would bemoan the fact that she never got the opportunity to attend college and become a teacher. For months I heard this story over and over. So one day as she was telling me this story for the umpteenth time, I thought about John Brown Russwurm. I said: "Tammy, why don't you stop talking about it and do it? Think about this house that we are seated in, named after the man who went to school here. Think about the types of indignities he had to face as a black man all those years ago. Yet, despite all his challenges, he went on to graduate from college. You need to find a way to make your dream a reality. Stop talking about the limitations. You can take out a student loan; you'll get a good job to pay it back when you graduate. You can get your mom to babysit your boys. You won't have to rely on this minimum-wage salary you're making right now or your husband for an allowance." I finished: "I'm really tired of hearing you cry and complain. Just do something about it!"

The school semester was coming to a close for summer. I went back home to work with welfare mothers on a back-to-work project sponsored by the U.S. government and earned money for the fall semester. When I returned for the next semester, I went back to the Afro-American center. It was a favorite meeting spot for black students on campus. I went to look for Tammy, and the director greeted me with a scowl as he informed me that Tammy had quit to go back to school. She had actually enrolled in a community college in a neighboring town. Tammy ended up as a teacher at this same community college a few years later.

Think about all of your childhood dreams, and even your adult ones. There are ways to overcome any obstacles that may be in your way. If you always wanted to write, start writing. If you always wanted to dance, take dance classes. That goes for cooking, piano or guitar, flower arranging, skydiving, interior decorating, or anything else you ever wanted to learn. Taking classes expands your horizons. If there is a particular career path you want to take and you don't have the academic credentials required, then enroll in college and take night classes if you have to. If you don't have the money, then take out a student loan. I did not have money at all to go to law school and borrowed most of it through student loan programs. Yep, I had to pay it back, but it was worth it because I am a judge now.

When people tell me, "You know, I always wanted to _____," I always respond with, "Fill in your blank and just do it. Stop dreaming!" Whatever you put in the blank, decide to make it happen despite whatever obstacles you may face. It's always worth it in the end.

—

"Goals are dreams with deadlines."
–DIANA SCHARF HUNT

V

CLEARER
SKIES
AHEAD

People are often unreasonable, illogical and self centered;
Forgive them anyway.

If you are kind, people may accuse you of selfish, ulterior motives;
Be kind anyway.

If you are successful, you will win some false friends and some
true enemies;
Succeed anyway.

If you are honest and frank, people may cheat you;
Be honest and frank anyway.

What you spend years building, someone could destroy
overnight;
Build anyway.

If you find serenity and happiness, they may be jealous;
Be happy anyway.

The good you do today, people will often forget tomorrow;
Do good anyway.

Give the world the best you have, and it may never be enough;
Give the world the best you have anyway.

You see, in the final analysis, it is between you and your God;
It was never between you and them anyway.

—MOTHER TERESA'S ANYWAY POEM

Developing Your Own Style

As a judge, I am often amazed at the way some folks dress for their day in court. Most appalling are the women. Women my own age! Their clothing has run the gamut from sleep caps, bedroom slippers, Daisy Dukes undershirts, and pajama pants, to even beach coverups! Being a judge requires me to look beyond presentation. But life is not a courtroom, and how you present yourself to the world determines how the world receives and perceives you and, ultimately, how it treats you. If you look like a floozy, you will be treated like one—by men and women alike. If you dress like you don't take yourself seriously, no one else will either. People pick up unspoken cues about you based on your appearance, rightfully or wrongfully.

One of the key principles involved in staying in your own lane is that you get to define how you want to represent yourself to others, which speaks to how you feel about yourself. I am a huge proponent of working on yourself by peeling away layers of "stuff" in order to arrive at who you really are and what type of life you want to live. Developing your sense of style is but an extension of this hard work. You have to decide what message you want your look to convey to the world. Is it one of confidence, approachability, seriousness, professionalism, or flirtatiousness? If so, you're in the right chapter of this book. If you want to dress like a strumpet and not be taken seriously, this section of the book is not for you.

Dressing appropriately gives me a certain amount of confidence and comfort to tackle the unknowns that each day may present, whether in my professional or personal life. Have you ever been in a situation where a lot of things you had not anticipated cropped up in your day and you couldn't fully focus on them because you weren't happy with the way you were put together? I have. It's distracting and doesn't allow you to fully and freely engage when you constantly have to pull down your skirt or hold in your stomach because your blouse is the wrong size. If you want your look to say, "I am a confident person at the wheel of my own life who knows where I have been and where I'm going," then you might want to consider some of the suggestions in this section.

Personal style is just that—personal. We develop it from experience, trial and error, and observing others whose styles we admire. That being said, America has become a country of imitators. There are entire magazine issues that focus on showing and telling you how to replicate the styles you see on celebrities, TV, and runways. I know they say "imitation is the sincerest form of flattery," but the trick is to pick out those things that you want to incorporate into your *own* presentation. You are not trying to walk around like you borrowed your entire wardrobe from some rock star.

I can't overstate how important it is to first take a long look in the mirror—and the closet—to assess how you come across. If you want to exude confidence and style, are those the words your wardrobe is saying to you, or is it some other word? The late designer Coco Chanel said: "Fashion fades; only style remains the same." I agree. Style has nothing to do with money or breeding. It's about how you carry yourself. It's about knowing what looks good on you and being confident enough in your choices to go anywhere in the world, knowing that you will be treated well because you demand it by your presence. You can do this regardless of the amount of money in your bank account. When I got my first job after law school, I earned $23,000 a year. Even back then, it was a paltry salary to live on. I learned to shop in thrift and consignment stores. I have campaigned for office in suits I bought at a thrift store, cross-examined the lead homicide detective in a murder case in red pumps I got at Goodwill, and appeared on CNN in a silk blouse I got on eBay for $12. Recently, I bought a pair of designer leather pumps in a new thrift store I discovered on my way to Walgreens. They are as cute as can be and appear to have never been worn. They cost $9! Some of the best pieces in my wardrobe are bargains I found in used clothing stores. There is no shame in my game and there shouldn't be any in yours. So take it from me, regardless of your financial circumstances, you have the ability to present yourself as a "class act with style."

My motto is, it's better to have ten quality items in your closet than to have fifty so-so items. I am neither a fashionista nor a personal stylist. My sense of style is a work in progress with plenty of room for improvement. But one thing I do know is that timeless clothes are always in fashion. When I look in my closet at the items that I have owned for years and that are still wearable and appropriate today, this is what I notice:

1. A tailored fitted jacket in a solid color is always in fashion. Take a look at movies down through the decades. You will often see a woman wearing a tailored blazer.
2. Solid colors are more lasting than prints. Patterns and prints change every season. Plaids and polka dots come and go, but black and beige are forever. So, a black cashmere sweater can be worn over and over with different outfits for years. I have two black cashmere sweaters I bought after law school that I still wear today.
3. Straight, knee-length skirts seem to have hung around for decades, whereas minis and maxis have come and gone.
4. Accessories change faster than clothing styles, so you can just use accessories to update your classic pieces.

I am not an authority on fashion. I decide bad fashion the way the Supreme Court decided what is pornographic and obscene: I know it when I see it! And the yellow mohair sweater that looks bad on Susie could look great on Barbara, which brings me to another thing. It is a challenge for a 250-pound middle-aged woman to carry off a cropped jean jacket. And it's equally difficult for a 5'1" woman to carry off a maxi dress. Remember that we want our clothes to say that we know quality and we know ourselves to be of quality.

Is your clothing clean? Stained and soiled clothes never, ever look good. They give the impression of sloppiness. It's not all that hard to make sure your clothes look fresh. You don't even have to spend a lot of money at the dry cleaners. There are products in the detergent aisle of your local grocer's that you can use to spot-remove stains and to dry clean at home. They are a great investment considering how much they'll save you on your cleaning bills. Not to mention the savings in not having to run around dropping off and picking up your clothes at the laundry. Beauty may be painful, but I am here to tell you that it need not be expensive.

Do your clothes show signs of wear? When you wear something that is dingy or threadbare, it gives the impression that you could not do better. Nope, tattered and faded clothes have got to go. As I said earlier, I could do TV commercials for Goodwill and other thrift stores. These places have some great clothes at rock-bottom prices. It is better to wear the same pair of slacks two days in a row with different shoes and accessories than to wear something that should be trashed just to give the impression that you have a lot to choose from in your closet.

Does your clothing fit? This is a really, really sticky subject for a lot of women, including myself. I have one friend who categorizes her clothes in her closet by size. From size 12 to size 18! Her closet represents the range of weight she has lost and gained over the years. She, like me, and maybe many of you, has battled weight issues for most of her adult life and the closet is just confirmation. Everyone is not fortunate enough to have the means to keep such an extensive wardrobe. But you can—and must—still look good at your present size, no matter what it is. I hate my big clothes too! I would much rather wear a size 12 than a 16. But the reality is that we look better in clothes that fit than in clothes that don't. If you've gotten a little bigger than you'd like, you just have to make peace with that fact and dress for the size you are. You'll look and feel much better and comfortable. And that's where undergarments come in. I have learned that, as with everything else in life, you have to start with the proper *foundation*. Please don't make the mistake a lot of women do in underestimating the importance of proper underwear. If your cup is running over, it'll show through that nice sweater you're wearing and take away from the flow of the fit. If your panties are too small, that line they make across your bottom will ruin any outfit. It will serve you well if you invest some time and a little money into shoring up your foundation. Pretty shapewear is out there for all shapes and sizes.

Just for fun, let me leave you with the following thought. When the weather is sunny and 80 degrees out, and everybody is outside having a good time, which would you prefer to drive: a clean and shiny Corvette convertible or the exact same Corvette covered in mud and dirt with trash and debris littering the floor ? Either way, it's a Corvette, right? But I bet you would choose the pretty, clean one. You would enjoy driving it and you would get a lot more attention in it. Create that same positive first impression in your presentation of yourself.

—

"Know, first, who you are; and then adorn yourself accordingly."
—EPICTETUS

Let Me Entertain You

When I plan an event, no matter how informal or small, I take great pains to make sure that I create an environment that is welcoming to everyone who has been invited. I am known in my crowd of friends for my parties, and have hosted everything from game night to bingo parties. I have thrown Halloween, Christmas, murder mystery, salsa dance, and masquerade parties. So I know what it takes to host a successful and memorable social event. And I do not believe you have to spend a lot of money to throw successful events, especially at home!

I was once invited to a fortieth birthday party. The invitation was beautiful. It was black with raised silver lettering and came inside a silver foil envelope. That classy invitation set the tone for my expectations. This is the first lesson in planning an event: The invitation, whether by email or snail mail, should create anticipation. I was familiar with the venue where the party would be held: the beachside lounge area of a small boutique hotel that looks like a beach house. Smart girl, I thought of the hostess. That is the second lesson: Choose a venue that has a festive atmosphere or create that type of aura in your home. But from the moment I arrived at the birthday party, I knew it was going to be a dull affair. Nothing looked like it had been planned at the actual venue. The presentation of the food was uninspiring; there were a bunch of chips and dip and finger food laid out haphazardly on a table. The bar was set up away from the lounge inside what looked like a large storage room. And while the decor was beautiful, the arrangement of sofas and tables was more appropriate for a large crowd, not for this more intimate affair. If there was music, I don't remember it. In sum, the event failed to live up to the promises implied by the invitation. I could see that I was not the only guest who felt disappointed.

When I got there, people were milling around not talking to one another and the hostess was sitting on a sofa in the corner talking with a friend. I had been there a good fifteen minutes before she even acknowledged me. She acted like a guest rather than a hostess. She had failed two final lessons. Lesson number three: Create an environment that is inviting and welcoming to your guests. And lesson number four: Be a good hostess by welcoming your guests and introducing them to others at the event. I was gone within half an hour, and a few other guests were heading to their cars along with me. This was not the first or the last time I have been to a party where I walked in and felt a vibe that made me want to turn around and go home. Have you felt that before? Social events are supposed to be fun. If not, why bother hosting one? If you want your guests to have fun, then you have to go the extra mile in making sure you have done your best to create a fun event. For all but the most impromptu gathering, some careful planning will enable you to relax and ensure that your guests enjoy a hospitable atmosphere.

The budget and theme: Start with your budget. The costs I use here are based on prices in Miami, which is really an expensive city. If you live in a city with a lower or higher cost of living, you can adjust your budget accordingly. If you know that you can afford to spend, say, $300, on your party, then you know what your parameters are going to be. You need to decide what type of party is appropriate for your budget. You cannot entertain a hundred people for $300 or throw an elaborate party with that sort of budget. A game night is one low-priced option. Having a theme for your event makes the atmosphere less intimidating, especially when your guests don't know one another. It can offer them something to talk about and makes them comfortable because they have something in common with one another. Game night is a good way to include everyone in what's happening, and once the games are over, because people were in a positive, fun situation together, the party can segue into dancing or lively conversation. As for the games, the best are the ones that require groups or teams. I like to include Taboo, Charades, Uno, Skipbo, Guesstures, and sometimes bid whist, for example. You want games that you can play at a quick, fun pace. Call your guests to find out if they have party games they can bring along too. Check out thrift stores for used games. I bought my murder mystery game on eBay for $6 with free shipping.

The guest list: Think about who you are going to invite to your party. Make a guest list. Will people be able to bring a date or friend if they are single? Make this clear in the invitation. Think of how your different friends fit in with one another. The good thing about having a game night is that it is the type of party that brings all types of personalities together. So you can feel confident inviting people who would hardly be compatible at, say, a sit-down dinner party. You can mix family and friends for game night and also include teenage children.

The invitation: Make sure you send your invitations out at least two weeks in advance to give your guests time to arrange their schedules. You don't want to be disappointed if you wait until the last minute and most of your intended guests have made other plans. How you invite people is important. Sending an invitation gives your guest a tangible reminder about your upcoming event. You can find some nice preprinted invitations for less than $10 at your local pharmacy or discount department store. I don't know about you, but I sure feel special these days when I get an invitation by U.S. mail. Imagine the tone it would set for your event if your intended guests got an invitation from you in the mail! But if you don't want to go through the added time and expense of paper invitations, you can always send electronic invitations.

The food: If I walk into one more party and see another cold chicken wing platter from the local supermarket, I swear I am going to scream! It is such a cop-out to order those platters. They seem to be everywhere. But, in keeping with the game night example, you are going to want to stick to finger food. It does not make sense to try to serve spaghetti and meatballs when people are going to be playing games and eating at the same time! My rule of thumb is to have two finger foods, one casserole-type dish, and a display of desserts. For 25 guests, this can easily be done for $125. That is $5 per guest! A casserole is a single dish that represents a complete meal. For example: chicken and rice, lasagna, southern cottage pie (made with hamburger and mashed potatoes, delicious!), or baked macaroni with sausage. This gives your guests something hot and filling instead of trying to load everyone up on finger foods. Have you ever been to a party with only finger food? Unless you had eaten beforehand, I bet you couldn't wait to get out of there to go get yourself a proper meal. To round out the food for your game night party, you need dessert. Buy a sheet cake, some nice cookies (those that come in round tin cans would be perfect because the different cookies sit in their own individual cups, which looks good on display), and individually wrapped chocolate candies.

Instead of serving cold appetizers, do yourself and your guests a favor and buy one of those prepackaged hot food preparation kits. They sell them in the bulk food stores. You get three aluminum trays (otherwise known as chafing dishes) with racks and cans of Sterno to keep the food warm. You can warm up to six separate dishes at a time. At this writing, that kit will cost less than $15. You can get drummettes in the frozen aisle of the grocer in large party-size bags. Also look for frozen meatballs, egg rolls, pigs in a blanket, and other bulk appetizers. You can prepare these foods the night before and have them warming on the chafing dishes by the time your guests arrive. You want to have as much fun as your guests, so prepare food ahead of the party.

A word about timing: How many times have you arrived at a party and the hosts are still setting up? That just irks me! I talk about setting up a little later on. But in line with this discussion, we need to talk about getting yourself some help. Don't depend on your friends and family for help. Hire help! Here is another secret I am going to share: It is cheap to hire professional help for your house party. Contact your local culinary school or community college about hiring a student who is studying hospitality to help with your party. Sure, you can line up your child or another young person, but they have not been trained in hospitality. They won't have the skills to take over the reins of the party logistics. Plus, they want to enjoy the party too. Culinary students learn about preparation, setup, presentation, and serving food. During Christmas 2009, I hosted a party, a near disaster by the way, because I had it on Christmas Eve and most people are doing last-minute shopping or trying to prepare for their own Christmas festivities on that night.

You live and learn. Anyway, I contacted the culinary school in town to inquire about help. How about I hire a young woman for $15 per hour? There was no minimum time required. So for a five-hour party, I paid $75. This helper came an hour before the party, and I told her how I wanted things set up, showed her where everything was, washed my hands of it, and went into my room to get dressed. During the party, she made sure the Sterno cans were burning, replenished the food and kept it looking enticing, picked up discarded dishes and cups, and even washed the dishes and cleaned the kitchen.

The drinks: This is where a party budget can get wiped out. Unless you are having a big bash like a wedding or large birthday, be smart about serving drinks. For $35 I purchased a plastic, but attractive, large beverage dispenser. I fill it with lemonade or iced tea or punch made from frozen concentrate. I usually choose a "signature cocktail," like cosmos or margaritas, and that is my only responsibility for alcohol. You can choose any signature cocktail you wish. Just make sure it is simple to make and something that can be done ahead of time. Oh, one final thing: buy two more bags of ice than you think you will need. Trust me on this. Nobody ever wants to volunteer to make an ice run if you run out of ice. Better safe than sorry.

Setting up: This may be the most crucial aspect of your party, but is most often overlooked. Take a look around your place. Is it user-friendly? Is the furniture set up in a way that makes it easy for people to walk around? Have you set up the area where the games are going to take place? Do you need to bring in chairs from the dining area or from your bedroom to make sure everybody will get a seat? Something I have done in the interest of protecting my furniture from spilled drinks and food is to cover all my furniture and chairs in white sheets. I went to a thrift store years ago and bought used white sheets for fifty cents apiece for this singular purpose. And there is something magical that happens in a room where you have covered everything in sheets of white. It starts to create the ambiance. I found this out by accident when I first used the white sheets. All of a sudden, my living room looked different and, somehow, more elegant. Have you seen the tall white candles inside glass tubes that they sell in the 99 cent stores? Buy yourself a dozen of those. Then dim the lights in strategic places such as the food table, your entryway, or a den where you might have guests just sitting and talking, and place your lighted candles in there. Make sure you put one in the bathroom too! You have now instantly and cheaply transformed your home into an intimate and inviting lounge. Candles and the white-covered furniture will make your home a thing of beauty that will be pleasing to the eye and the spirit.

I make bouquets from branches and blooms in my garden. I thought this was something only people in the tropics could do until I spent two months in St. Louis in the winter with my brother and nephew, where I saw shrubs and bushes with little red berries in his yard that could easily be commissioned for party decor. You just have to use your imagination. Check out home decor magazines for other economical ideas for setting the party mood in your surroundings. I always start setting up my house a few days before my event. Spending one hour a night in the days before your party preparing your home pays off big-time in the end and helps alleviate last-minute stress.

I set up my food and drink tables the night before I have an event so that I can check it off my list for party day preparations. I want to be fresh and not frazzled by the time the party gets under way. You want to be stress-free too. When setting up, take some time to think about innovative ways to display your food. I have used brightly colored sheets and bedspreads as tablecloths for my buffet table. Set out your plates and utensils in fun and inspiring ways by using baskets for napkins and interesting containers or tall glassware for the forks and knives. Dessert tables are the most fun. I "layer" my dessert table to make it more interesting by using large books (dictionaries and children's books are great for this purpose) to create platforms of varying heights. For our game night dessert table, I created two platforms of different heights with the books, then covered the entire table with a tablecloth or sheet. Then I set out three different platters with a cake on the table surface itself, cookies on one platform nicely arranged in their cups, and wrapped candy in a bowl on the other platform. Add candles and you have taken the ordinary into the realm of the extraordinary. With every party I throw, I see my creativity expanding. If you take the time and use your imagination when it comes to the presentation of food and drinks, you will be tapping into creative energy you may not have known you have. It is worth it for yourself and for your guests. Think of the difference between the cheap Chinese food buffets and five-star hotel buffets. There really isn't a big difference in the food they are offering. As with most things in life, it's all in the presentation!

My final word on this entire subject has to do with hosting your event. I am assuming that you have already set the mood with decor and presentation. The most unforgettable parties begin and end with a good hostess who welcomes and engages each and every one of her guests. Many people forget about this element of a successful party. If you have planned everything in advance, then you will be available to enjoy the party right along with your guests. The reason I write about entertaining is because I believe that playing hostess allows a woman to tap into her creative energy as well as building up her confidence. It teaches you to be gracious and sharpens your conversation skills. These are all benefits that brighten your journey and add spice to your life. What type of hostess are you?

"Trifles make perfection, and perfection is no trifle."
–UNKNOWN

Old-fashioned Common Courtesy

The world would be a better place for everyone if we started thinking about what it means to be considerate and gracious. It's a challenge to comport ourselves with a high standard of decency, to do what is right and honorable, when we see so much meanness and indecency going on around us, especially on TV and in the behavior of celebrities and would-be role models.

When I was a child, my uncle drove several of my cousins and me to the beach in the back of his truck. It was a big truck, a flatbed usually used to haul animals, hay, and produce, the kind with the big wooden slats on the side. I told you Miami was the south. We use to stand up in the flatbed in the back and hold on to the cab of the truck as we drove over the high bridge that connects the city of

Miami to the Key Biscayne beaches. They don't let children do that stuff anymore. Maybe it's a good thing, but we never had a mishap. Anyway, my uncle stopped at a neighborhood corner store to buy drinks and ice before we headed to the blacks-only beach, Virginia Key. As we were waiting for my uncle out in the hot sun, a lady in the house in front of which we had parked came out with a tray full of cookies and a pitcher of sweet iced tea. I guess she saw us sweating in the back of that old truck and felt sorry for us. She was such a sweet little old lady. I still remember her face, and I am cringing now in embarrassment as I write this story. She passed out these cookies and then she stood there smiling at us as we ate. I must have been seven or eight years old. I didn't like the cookies, but I didn't say anything. Not at first. But then she offered to put the rest of them in a paper bag for us to take to the beach, and that is when I blurted out, "Yuck, no, we don't want any more. They're dry," and the next thing out of my big mouth was, "and you didn't put enough sugar in 'em." She stammered something about having run out of sugar and apologized for them being dry. My uncle came back out and we headed on out to the beach. We had a great time that day.

Later on that evening when I got home I told my mother about the incident with the cookie lady. She was aghast! She was mortified about the words I had said to this to nice lady whom I didn't know and who had brought us cookies and sweet tea out of the kindness of her heart. My mom said: "You should have told her they were delicious and thanked her. When she offered the rest of them to you,

you should have taken them with a smile and said another thank you. But instead, you were fresh! You hurt her feelings when all she was doing was being nice to you. You could have thrown the cookies away later. That would have been better than hurting her feelings. I didn't raise you that way." I felt very guilty for a long time about how I must have made that lady feel. I had nightmares that she never baked cookies again. That she was crying herself to sleep at night for baking those dry, sugarless cookies that nobody wanted. Or worse, that she started being mean and hateful to little children because I made her realize how selfish and ungrateful we are.

Children do say hurtful things, and that's one reason we teach them good manners. A French poet once said, "Good manners require space and time." With space and time, I have learned better behavior and social skills. In short, I have had to learn to mind my manners. These are the little sacrifices we make that make life pleasant for us and for those who have to interact with us. What good did it do to tell the old woman that the cookies were awful? She wasn't a contestant in a baking competition; she was trying to be a good Samaritan. I have since accepted cookies, cakes, clothes, shoes, bottles of wine, and even living room furniture—all things I didn't like—so as not to hurt the feelings of the giver. There is always a charity that needs most of these things, so I don't mind much.

We all know that the world today is more stressful than ever. People have financial worries, and they have concerns about their children's futures, identity theft, adequate health care, and keeping their jobs. In this fast-paced, stressful environment, good manners are taking a backseat to other considerations, and people are behaving more poorly than ever in public. Take cell phone usage for example. I was just standing in line the other day at the pharmacy waiting to pay for my purchases, and the customer in front of me was deeply involved in a conversation on her cell phone. She had a cart full of stuff that she was loading onto the counter while she continued her phone conversation, searched the bottom of her purse for coupons, and talked to the sales clerk, all at the same time. The rest of us in the growing checkout line were tapping our feet with impatience. I was definitely at *my* wits' end. I gently tapped her on the shoulder and said "Excuse me, ma'am, but you need to hang up the phone." She turned and looked at me with her mouth opened in surprise and then I said, "Hang up the phone, please." With a shamefaced expression, she told whomever she was talking to that she had to go and then she quickly hung up. She then said to me: "I'm sorry, I was talking to my daughter. She calls me ten times a day. I guess she's bored." I replied "But you don't have to answer ten times. Maybe you're bored too. " She looked at me in shock, but I meant every word. I guess you think I had to have some pretty big pink balls to tell her that, but she was crossing into my lane by being disrespectful of my time. It is a matter of courtesy, manners, and respecting the rights of others when you turn off your cell phone. I have seen people talking on their phones during luncheons with their friends. This common practice is disrespectful to the person who took time out of their lives to devote some time to you. You owe that friend, colleague, or family member your undivided attention.

Another area where I see unbridled rudeness is in the way some deal with people whose job it is to serve the public. Sales clerks, government personnel, bus drivers, and waiters are people who have public relations jobs. I have witnessed restaurant patrons cursing and swearing at their servers. I have seen people throwing temper tantrums at the DMV, being rude to flight attendants, and even witnessed a fight inside a fast-food restaurant between the order taker and a customer. I used to think good manners was about making others feel good, but I have come to realize, from personal experience, that having good manners is about making ourselves feel good. When you hold the door for someone struggling with a baby stroller, or help an elderly person bring in his groceries, or give your seat up to someone with a handicap, doesn't that make you feel good? When we treat others with respect, we are respecting ourselves. When we degrade and belittle another person, we also take ourselves down a couple of notches in *our own* estimation of ourselves. I use to be guilty of this behavior myself.

Once when I was in law school, I got so angry at a teller in a bank that I ended up screaming at the top of my lungs and calling her everything but a child of God. Then I stormed out of the crowded bank in a huff, leaving a cloud of negative energy behind me. I felt so justified in my tirade. The teller had refused to cash a check because my identification was expired. *I* had let *my* identification expire, but I felt justified telling this lady about herself. But something inside of me didn't feel okay with how I had behaved. As I replayed the incident in my mind, I realized that the way I treated that woman left me feeling powerless and out of control. I didn't walk out of the bank with the money from the check. So how did I win? My only success was in creating a scene that could easily have resulted in my arrest or permanent banishment from the bank. In losing control of myself, I lost control of my ability to resolve the situation amicably. And it got me absolutely nowhere.

There are ways to get our needs met without resorting to public cursing and/or violence. My mother always says, "You can catch more flies with honey than with buttermilk." I was pouring buttermilk a lot, but then it dawned on me that when I had an unpleasant experience with someone in a supermarket, or customer service, or a department store, it not only left me with raised blood pressure, it left me feeling bad about myself and it left me feeling powerless to effect positive results. And I was making myself look bad to boot. The turning point for me came when I had to deal with a clerk in a department store who was giving me major attitude. My first impulse was to match her attitude. But before I could utter one, "Wait a minute, Missy," a thought occurred to me. Her name tag was on her shirt. I said very calmly and softly, "Janet, would you mind calling the manager over, please?" She wasn't expecting that. Maybe she was used to customers shouting: "WHERE'S THE MANAGER"? She could handle that, because it sounded like fighting words. My calm, no-nonsense tone brought down her irritation too. Cooler heads really do prevail. Janet spoke back to me softly. Then she changed her position on the matter of contention and offered to help me.

When you're angry and indignant, you are really operating from a point of weakness. Anger triggers our "fight-or-flight" impulses. Neither is a good impulse to have when all you want is the size nine pair of pumps in blue, not beige. Since that day with Janet, I do not get into arguments or shouting matches with people in the service industry. I speak calmly, no matter what. And if I am not getting the results I expect, I simply ask for the manager. This method has worked for me like a charm. Another benefit is that it has made my life journey a lot more pleasant. That's not to say that I don't come up against irate people, but I resist the temptation to match their attitude and energy. I do it for myself, not for them.

You can change your interactions in this world too. You don't know what kind of stress or personal pressures the people you encounter in the public sector or at work may be experiencing. But you have the power to set the tone for your interactions. Don't try changing the world, try changing yourself, and your world will miraculously change too.

Does it seem that you are embattled in just about every area of your life? That your interactions with people more often than not end in conflict? Stop and ask yourself how it all makes you feel. You have power over your experience in this life, not someone else outside of you. Staying in your lane means having your eye on every aspect of YOUR life. On the parts that are working as well as those areas that aren't working. I invite you, in all of your interactions, to take the path that honors the wonderful soul that you are.

"It's nice to be important, but it's more important to be nice."
–JOHN CASSIS

You Can See the World

Ever since I was a little girl I have enjoyed reading. My dad said I talked before I crawled and I read before I walked. And my favorite books were those with pictures of faraway places. As a result, I developed a yearning to travel at a young age. It really is no wonder. My mind is always in constant motion, so I guess it makes sense that I like to "go" too. There is something about traveling that energizes the spirit and mind. I believe that everyone should travel whenever they get the chance. You learn how people think and live in different parts of the world.

I traveled to Morocco in 2003, only two years after the World Trade Center disaster. My friends and I ended up in this town called Fez, which has a majority Muslim population with Jews and Christians rounding out the rest. My only experience with Muslims was what I saw on the news and with the ones in the Middle Eastern–run stores in the black communities. In Fez, we stayed in a house that was run by a Muslim named Ali. He was very friendly. One night during dinner he shared his feelings about the image the world had of people who practiced Islam. He felt humiliated that there were people in the world who viewed him personally, and Muslims generally, as terrorists. He said that once someone learned he was a Muslim, they assumed he was a fanatic hell-bent on the destruction of the western world. It helped me realize that my own feelings about racial stereotyping as a black person were no different from what many Muslims may have been feeling. Traveling and meeting Ali broadened my understanding of a culture I had no direct contact with. I doubt that I would have grown in my perspective had I not traveled to this Muslim country on the tip of north Africa.

When I suggest that you think about traveling, I'm not talking about trips that deplete your bank account. I don't believe in spending a fortune to travel. And life is too short to wait until you can "afford" to travel. Sometimes, opportunities to get away are right in your own city. I meet people born and raised in Miami who have never been to the Everglades, or the Museum of Science, or the Seaquarium. I lived for a while in Brooklyn directly across the street from the Brooklyn Botanic Garden. I read somewhere that if Brooklyn were its own city, it would be the second-largest city in the country. The humanity and noise can sometimes be overwhelming. Don't get me wrong, I love Brooklyn. But whenever the people and the noise got too much for me to take, I would go over to the garden, a 52-acre sanctuary of beauty and peace with more than 10,000 species of plant life from around the world. Once inside, it was hard to imagine that you were surrounded on all four sides by one of the most populated cities on earth. And the garden was usually deserted. Very few people were ever there. I remember many times taking my lunch and sitting next to the waterfall of the Japanese garden exhibit. And I would be the only person there!

I use to have a weekly card party at my house just about every Friday with five or six of my close friends about twenty-five years ago. We were all young, starting out in our careers, and we didn't have a lot of money. So we would all chip in $5 each to buy the party provisions, which were usually the same thing: chili dogs, chips, cookies or cake, and a big jug of cheap wine. Such a simple menu. But those card parties were some of the happiest and most memorable moments of my life back then. I had a great group of friends. In fact, the camaraderie that I shared with these friends led me to seek new ways to enjoy life with them. On the road!

During this time, I started taking long drives—I called them "sanity drives," which I still take today—to get away from noise, obligations, and pressures. I take them to think. I turn the radio and my cell phone off and I sometimes talk to God. No matter where you live, there is a beautiful drive somewhere near you. You can drive through small towns, along a river, through a desert or mountains, or along historic trails. Recently, I had to visit a part of my county to which I rarely go, got lost down a road, and found a beautiful park with a lake. I got out of my car and sat by the lake to watch the butterflies and birds. I had been feeling stressed-out in the morning because I was trying to meet some deadlines, but finding that park and taking the time to spend a moment enjoying nature allowed me to gather my thoughts and reenergize my spirit.

When you take a drive, avoid major highways and expressways and look for the back roads if possible. When I started taking my drives, I really didn't know much about Florida, the state that I grew up in. So I found travel books in the library and learned about different areas of the state, and took day trips to these places. If it was too far away for a day trip, I found a cheap hotel and stayed overnight. It was during one such drive that I discovered Marco Island, Florida. It is about 90 miles west of Miami off a one-lane stretch of road called the Tamiami Trail through the Everglades. Back then, Marco was a little-known hamlet off the beaten path, and when I drove out of the Everglades and over the high bridge and down into this small island on the Gulf of Mexico, I fell in love. It looked like a place out of a travel magazine. That is when the idea came to me that maybe my friends from the Friday card group would like to spend a weekend there.

We couldn't afford to pay much money to stay at a nice place on the beach in Marco so I set about doing my research. I learned about a hotel on the island that had two-bedroom apartments on the beach. For two nights, we could rent an apartment for four hundred dollars. Divided among six people, that was less than $70 per person. Well, even $70 was a lot of money for us. So we all agreed to save ten dollars a week over the next couple of months to pay for the trip. It was worth the sacrifice because, I tell you, we had an absolute ball the weekend we went to Marco! We bought groceries and each took turns preparing our meals. We hung out at the beach and in the pool and Jacuzzi, and at night, we played cards and board games and laughed and joked. Yep, it was a great trip. And it was the first of several trips that I have taken over the last thirty years with my friends.

We have since traveled to Jamaica, Barbados, Kenya, and Spain, to name just a few places. And we have always done it the same way. Somebody suggests a place. We figure out the budget to travel to that place. (We always try to rent a house or villa—more about that later.) One of the friends collects the money from everybody in monthly installments and deposits it in a bank account. Our second trip as a group was to Jamaica. I thought it would be great to rent a villa. In Jamaica and other places in the Caribbean, South America, and Mexico, you can rent a large house that comes with a staff, including a cook, butler, and housekeeper. If you are traveling as a group, I promise you that staying in a villa is cheaper and a lot more fun than staying at a hotel or resort. It makes you feel like a native. You can come down to breakfast in your pajamas, or swim in the pool by yourself, and you will have much more personal space to spread out.

As we were waiting to board the plane to Montego Bay,

there was another group of people who came from New York waiting to board also. It turns out they were all long-time girlfriends and had reservations at a resort in Negril. They were so excited and giggly because this was their first trip to Jamaica and the first time they were traveling as friends. They had been saving up for a year to take this trip and it cost the six of them $900 apiece for the entire vacation, including airfare—$5,400 in total.

At the end of that week, I saw the same group of women from New York at the Montego Bay airport waiting to board their flight back to the U.S. They all looked very glum, and the group had shrunk in number. I asked one of the women about their vacation. She said: "Two of my friends went home early. They were disappointed in the resort. The rooms were small and eating out was too expensive. Actually none of us really had a great time. We ending up arguing a lot. And we are barely speaking to one another now! I will never travel with this bunch again."

The four-bedroom villa we rented was right on the ocean with a private beach, pool, and tennis court, and it came with a car and driver. All for the grand total of $2,700. One member of our group had flown in from New York and her ticket had cost less than $300. Had those girlfriends from New York rented a similar villa, they would have had money left over, which they could have used to buy groceries for their one-week stay.

We felt like celebrities in our luxury villa. We had not one, but two world-class chefs who presented our meals with the artistry and flair that you only see at five-star resorts. Our butler served us coffee every morning on the oceanfront patio and cocktails every afternoon as we lounged by our pool. The house was equipped with games and movies, but we spent most of our time out on our private beach, or on the tennis court, or sightseeing in the van we had with the driver. One night, we even had a bonfire out on the beach.

You just don't get all that in a hotel. For me, renting a villa or house is the only way to go, and *you* can travel that way too! I wish I could show you some of the pictures of the places we've stayed—you'd be amazed. There are hundreds of websites that offer villa rentals around the world, and the prices are the lowest during off-season months. Take it from me, you just have to be smart about your choices. And one last tip about villa rentals that I've discovered over the years: You may want to bring along some staple foods such as canned tuna, peanut butter, cereal, etc. Purchasing these foods in island countries can be very expensive if you are able to find them at all. So if you're going to crave it, take it. On one of our trips, a girlfriend even brought a canned ham! We just couldn't leave the pork at home.

Check out online travel auction and bidding sites. You can get wonderful places for a steal. Last winter, I bid on a one-bedroom oceanfront apartment rental on the beach in Palm Beach County, Florida. I won the auction and paid $295 total (including taxes!) for the entire week. Other guests had paid that amount per night! I have vacationed numerous times this way, by bidding on travel auctions. I went to Buenos Aires, Argentina, for a week by winning a trip at auction for $600, which included airfare, hotel, breakfast daily, a city tour, and a tango lesson! How about that!? In 2008, in celebration of the Chinese year of the rat, as was the year of my birth, I bid on a trip to Hong Kong. I won the trip for $750, which included airfare from Miami to Hong Kong and six nights in a hotel. That is less than the cost of airfare alone.

Over my years of traveling, I have seen some great places and had a lot of fun building and renewing friendships while also gaining cultural awareness and sensitivity. And getting away from the everyday stresses and demands of my career also gives me quiet time for spiritual renewal. Traveling is more than just sightseeing. It is about building memories and experiences with friends and other loved ones.

You owe it to yourself to explore your world! Ready, Set, Go!

"Travel is fatal to prejudice, bigotry, and narrow-mindedness."
—MARK TWAIN

Your Second Act

There is a photo I used to have that my youngest brother took of me when I was twenty-four years old. I was sitting under the mango tree in our family's backyard smoking. My hair, a shocking shade of purple, was standing up everywhere on my head as though I had stuck my finger into an electric socket. I am sitting with my feet crossed, relaxed and looking like I don't have a care in the world, and surrounded by a cloud of smoke. My brother calls that photo "Purple Haze." Whenever I see that picture I am reminded of how God continually opens doors of opportunity for second chances to all of us. You see, that photo represents a time in my life when I had lost my way and parked my car on the side of the road to nowhere. I was nearly two years out of college, working temporary or low-paying jobs, and spending my money shopping, partying, and hanging out late at night with my friends. You could not believe how far off course my mind had strayed from my dreams. I was no longer interested in being successful. I had grown comfortable living a life of mediocrity. For as long as I can remember, I had been intelligent and ambitious, with big plans and dreams for my life. Yet, for nearly two years in the 1980s, I was spinning my wheels, going nowhere fast. I was satisfied with a life of sleeping late, drinking, and late-night parties. But I want you to know that I am living proof that it is never, ever too late for your second act. That no matter how far off course you've veered, you can turn your car around!

When I first graduated from college, I applied to the one law school that I had always wanted to attend: University of Chicago. But instead of getting accepted, I was placed on a waiting list. When I didn't get admitted, I applied again for the following year. While I waited the first year, I found a job as the director for a government-funded welfare-to-work program called CETA. I really enjoyed working to help the women in that program get back on their feet. They had fascinating stories, and their desire to become self-sufficient and financially independent was awesome to me. And though I was helping women get themselves out of a rut, I hadn't realized that I had fallen into one of my own. After about a year, the program ran out of funding and I had to look for another job. I was also rejected again from the University of Chicago. My dream started to dim.

I soon found myself in a series of short-lived menial jobs.

I stuffed envelopes for a financial services firm but lost that job when the company directors were indicted for fraud; I moved on to work for a manufacturer of restaurant kitchen equipment, but lost that job when the company's Miami division closed down after our boss, a seemingly nice man, was caught embezzling several hundreds of thousands of dollars; after that I worked as a telephone operator in the complaint department of a major retail chain, but lost that job when the chain was downsized by the larger retail chain that bought it; and then I found another job as a sales clerk in JCPenney's hosiery department. The reason I lost that job was entirely my own fault. I continually missed work. By the time I was working at JCPenney, I had developed a horrible work ethic. I was choosing to hang out every day at the beach with my friends and making up all sorts of excuses to my manager as to why I could not come into the store.

Well, one Tuesday I sashayed into work. I was in a great mood and wore a bright smile. I had enjoyed a three-day weekend of partying with my boyfriend and friends. My manager called me into his office and asked me where I had been the day before. I answered him, "Well, Mondays are always slow here, and it was such a beautiful day yesterday, I decided to spend it at the beach. It was too pretty a day to work." He replied, "You're fired." His response was not what I had anticipated at all! I sat there in total disbelief. How dare he!!! Then I said: "I work very hard here and I have many loyal customers on my mailing list. I'm smart and friendly and work overtime whenever it's requested of me. I come to work the majority of the time and, when I do, I am always on time." My view of the situation made perfect sense to me. I guess you can see how my devil-may-care attitude had seriously clouded my thinking and judgment. And I had taught "employability skills" to women trying to become self-sufficient! Looked like I needed to learn a few lessons myself. I was thoroughly ashamed of myself. That was the only job I have ever been fired from. To this day, whenever I go into JC Penney I am reminded of that fact.

It was around this time that my brother snapped the picture of me smoking in the backyard. My other brother, the older of my two brothers but younger than me, was home for a college break. He was attending the University of Florida studying to be a nuclear engineer. He asked: "Karen, when are you going to law school? I am tired of our friends asking me what you're doing with your life and telling them you're going to law school. It's been nearly two years since you've graduated from college. You're just going from job to job without a plan." I will never forget that day as long as I live. I was the oldest of the five of us and had set the pace and the bar for my younger siblings; I was the big sister who was class valedictorian and was looked up to by everyone. But when I looked at my brother's face that day, all I saw was disappointment. The look in his eyes made me realize that I had let him and my entire family down by my actions and inaction. I replied defensively, "But I want to go to the University of Chicago." He reminded me that I had been saying that for too long too. He said, "We are Florida residents. It's summer now, so you still have time to meet

the deadline for the spring session at the University of
Florida. Why don't you apply?" So I filled out the applica-
tion. I was admitted for the spring term, which began in
January. I had four months to get ready for school and life
in Gainesville, Florida. Instead of spending that time working harder to save money, I kept being trifling. Subcon-
sciously or consciously, I didn't want to go.

I couldn't admit to anybody, not even to myself, that I
really wanted to stay home. I had a boyfriend who I didn't
want to lose and friends who I liked hanging out with. I
didn't have to pay rent to live at home, and all was right with
the world. I was scared of things changing. I had grown
comfortable with what was familiar and safe. I didn't know
what to expect in Gainesville. My brother came home again,
this time for Christmas break, and I told him that I had saved
no money, I wasn't going to receive financial aid from the
university, and I did not trust my car to make the long trip
up to Gainesville. I was hoping he would say, "Well, why
don't you just wait and go next fall then?" My destiny was
opening up before me but I was standing with my back to it,
longing to stay in the comfort zone of the dead-end dirt road
I was trapped on. And there was my brother, ignoring my
excuses and gently directing me to make a U-turn. He said:
"Let's go. You can live with me, find a job. Buy used books.
We'll make a way. Just ... let's ... go!" I was still teetering.
God does not Himself appear as an apparition before us, He
sends angels. Here was a tow truck that God had sent for me
in the form of my brother, offering to pull me back onto the
road and onto solid ground. With my brother's pleading

ringing in my ear, I took a reluctant turn toward that tow truck.

We left Miami in my twenty-five-year-old Volvo. I used to name my cars back then. They were all old cars. I had a Baby Jane and a Foxy Lady. The Volvo's name was "Precious." As for finances, I am willing to raise my right hand under oath and swear to this truth: I had only twenty dollars to my name. My parents were worried about us trying to make the trip to Gainesville in Precious. She needed a new transmission, the engine overheated, the radiator leaked coolant, and the gas gauge didn't work so you never knew when you were low on fuel. We set off in the middle of the night anyway, on faith, driving Precious. I was quietly praying the whole way. I secretly wanted the car to break down so I would have to return home. I wanted another excuse to delay law school. It's a five-hour trip to Gainesville. Precious was a real champ that night. She didn't overheat or run out of gas or break down on some lonely stretch of highway. As you come off the exit ramp into Gainesville, there is a lone traffic light there. We could see that steady welcome beacon blinking as we exited the interstate. Precious made it to that traffic light and then died right there. Though I never drove that car again, she had let me off in the very place I needed to be in order to further a lifelong dream. I had finally arrived at law school.

Remember, God does *not* appear to us as a vision with wings. He guides us and answers our prayers in the form of the people He places in front of us. Listen to the people who love you. They are the angels God has placed alongside your life. They are the ones there to give you a jump-start when you need one. They are the ones there to take over the wheel when your life has spun out of control. If you believe that you have gotten off at the wrong exit, you can double back. There is someone to help you. You just have to ask Him in prayer. The answers will come in the words and actions of people who care about you. And sometimes the answers come from strangers. But they always come if you just listen with your ears and with your heart. Is it time for your act two?

—

"It is never too late to be what you might have been."
–George Eliot

Weight a Minute!

I thank God for giving me the wisdom, strength and drive to overcome just about every obstacle and personal challenge that has met me on this road of life. But there is one pitfall I have not been able to avoid. It has been for me a singular and never-ending problem. It is the personal war I have waged against fat. It pains me to admit that I have not been able to get a handle on my love handles. Since the age of twenty-one, I have either been thinking about a diet, on a diet, kind of on a diet, cheating on a diet, looking for a new diet, or thinking about looking for a new diet. Any woman with a weight problem can relate to this. I have done the grapefruit, cabbage soup, Mayo Clinic, vegetarian, hard-boiled egg, cookie, three-meal-a-day, lemonade, starvation, and Monday-is-a-brand-new-day diet. In frustration I have called Jenny and made appointments with Dr. Atkins. I have lost and I have gained and I have lost and I have gained in a vicious cycle of losing and gaining. The sizes in my closet are like roll call: 10 is here, 16 is here, 14 is here, 12 is here.

This battle hasn't gotten any easier with age. But one thing has changed drastically for me. It is the way I look at dieting, weight, and body image. And it came to me at a time when I wasn't paying attention to my weight. When I look at pictures of me at age twenty-six and age thirty-two, or age forty, I look perfectly fine. But at those different ages, even though I was thin, I didn't feel fine. I felt overweight. When I visited my brother for a two-month period while working on this book, he brought out pictures from a trip we took to Vermont when I was thirty-two years old. I was shocked when I saw myself in those pictures. I look emaciated. My neck is so small it looks like it can't hold the weight of my head. I look unhealthy. And I remember that I was terribly unhappy and lacked confidence and direction at that time. But I was not fat! But on that Vermont trip, I was watching my weight. I was striving to be thinner and thinner, trying to reach what I now realize was an unacceptable body weight for a woman of my height. Looking at those pictures got me to thinking about my weight issues throughout my adult life. I know now that I was never really overweight until about five years ago. And these last five years have been the most fulfilling of my life! Here I was, 60 pounds heavier than I had ever been in my life and yet, for the first time, I was in a place where I was truly happy with myself.

This peace came from learning to love and be happy with who I am. It came from being gentle with myself and treating myself as well as I would a baby. Every one of us has to learn this lesson. We must happily and with open arms grow to embrace the totality of the person that we are. Whatever that self is: the funny, smart, opinionated, sympathetic, creative, pigheaded, egotistical, personable, ornery, temperamental, sensitive, etc., self that we are needs to be celebrated and accepted and loved. I do not believe that I loved myself when I was a yo-yo dieter. I was never good enough for me. I was hard on me. I tried to please everyone. You can't please anybody if you aren't pleasing yourself. I used to believe that being thin would make me happy, but I was no happier thin than fat.

When I was big, my life was also its fullest. I was definitely overweight, but my life was working for me. I was traveling more and making new friends, taking Spanish classes and learning salsa and playing tennis, throwing parties, planning summer fun with my nieces and nephews, tending to my garden, and making a sanctuary of my home. I was not thinking about my weight one bit. I was fat and I was happy. My closest friends and one of my brothers all commented after the first two years of my weight gain that I was letting my weight get out of hand. In the past, those comments would have upset me, but I simply kept on eating, all the while agreeing with them that I should probably go on a diet. And I didn't start a diet for another two years, not a one. Then I got a court show. All of a sudden I was on television and I started seeing pictures of me posted on the Internet. That is when I, still slowly, began to realize how much weight I had gained in the past three or four years. One of my girlfriends who hadn't seen me in years said, "You don't even look like yourself." And looking at myself in the "Judge Karen" promo pictures, I realized she was right. It finally dawned on me that I had gained enough pounds to create a small child. Yet this revelation did not depress me as it would have in the past when a ten-pound weight gain would send me spiraling into a dark place where I would stop socializing until I had lost the pounds. This time was different. There was no shame in my game. I agreed with my friends that I needed to get serious about my health and my weight. They were really pressuring me!!!! But I was happy, despite my weight. I had spent the past few years focusing on creating my best life by seeking outlets that satisfied my soul and enhanced the quality of my spiritual, social, and family life.

Right now, I am being mindful of my eating habits and am taking walks and working out, even though I absolutely hate it! I decided I needed to lose weight because I want to move better on the tennis court and on the dance floor. I decided I needed to lose weight because I want to be able to wear some of the great vintage dresses hanging in my closet that are growing even more vintage. I decided I want to live a long life so I can be there for my family, which loves and needs me, especially my nieces and nephews.

And I decided I needed to lose the weight because I want to look better in the pictures that get plastered on the Internet without my permission. I wholly and totally accept the fact that the self that I love is also vain!

I know there will be setbacks. But as long as I operate from a place of self-love and remain gentle with myself, the weight loss is the candle on the cake I have already put icing on. If you are struggling with a weight problem, believe me, I feel your pain. I truly believe that you can and will overcome the obstacle of weight when you start to pay attention to other areas of your life that need attention. You should begin by working to make your dreams a reality, surrounding yourself with positive and supportive friends, and treating yourself with kindness. A whole new world of opportunities will begin to open up to you once your life starts heading in a positive direction. From this new position of power you can decide whether you want to become leaner or healthier, or you may decide that you are perfectly happy just the way you are. Whatever you do, do it from a place of self-love.

■—

"You can never, ever, use weight loss to solve problems that are not related to your weight. Losing weight is not a cure for life."
–Phillip C. McGraw

Weight a Minute Too!

My oldest niece, Veronica, collaborated with me on this book. They say youth is wasted on the young, but Veronica is a smart young woman who is learning to make beneficial choices for her life. She is learning from the mistakes of others rather than having to learn through mistakes of her own. Smart girl! At twenty-three years old, she is waging her own battle against unnecessary weight. During the course of writing this book, she has lost more than fifty pounds and still counting. I am very proud of her tenacity and resolve to live her best life by getting healthier and leaner for the journey ahead of her. She has been a great inspiration for me, and I wanted her to share her own story here, in her own words.

Last winter I was out shopping for a coat and passed a huge lady wearing the same outfit as me. I did a double take when I realized that I was passing a full-length mirror and that woman was me. I hardly recognized myself! It was almost like seeing a caricature of myself in a fun-house mirror. At twenty-three, I was almost double the weight I had been my freshman year of college.

I have always felt very beautiful and intelligent, but my weight has always been on my mind. One day my mother and I argued about whether I was thin in high school; she swore I never was. So she pulled out the photos, and there I was, so skinny my cheekbones were protruding from my face. That is how twisted the perception of weight was for me. Even when I was in shape I couldn't see it.

In my home, we had to ask permission to go in the fridge or fix a meal. My sister could eat the sweet treats and second helpings that I couldn't because I was heavier. Food developed an allure for me that restriction made even more intense. In middle school I would give my friends money to buy snacks to bring me the next day in class. Once I spent the day with my grandmother and she let me have two of my favorite cookies, and my mother stopped speaking to me for days for eating them. I believe I developed such an unhealthy relationship with food because it was seen as such a difficult prize to attain.

At thirteen my doctor told me I could stand to lose a bit of weight. She spoke to me about incorporating fruits and vegetables into my diet and a bit more exercise. That was the best advice I had ever gotten about getting healthy, and I didn't feel any negative pressure. I woke up early every morning and did aerobics and got into the best shape of my adolescent life. When I turned fourteen I stopped really eating. I would eat one sandwich when I came home from school. Then a friend of mine encouraged me to start eating again and once that started I couldn't stop, because I really do love food! I moved in with my Aunt Karen and I learned the art of dieting. She knows every diet ever invented by man or woman. Then one of my best friends taught me to throw up after my meals and that is how I really learned to balance my weight. I went through minilosses and gains but maintained a decent weight throughout high school, though there was part of me that didn't feel right unless I was starving. And throwing up created more problems than it solved.

My freshman year of college I exercised every day and was the happiest with my weight that I had ever been. I looked and felt amazing. Then I got on a new medication and gained thirty pounds in three months. I couldn't exercise anymore because I got a job and no longer had the time. Gaining so much weight in such a short amount of time really knocked me off-kilter. But I still kind of expected it to fall off when I got used to the medication. Over the next three years my weight slowly increased. When I was about seventy pounds overweight I began to exercise, and the weight did not move at all. I felt like I was restrained in a fat suit and the zipper was stuck. I got discouraged, and it was easier to gain weight than to lose it, so I gave up. I think that happens to a lot of women. I have seen it happen to some of my friends. It just all gets too hard sometimes. Every now and then I would try different diets but could never stick to them; I just wasn't willing to sacrifice the time, effort, or sanity to eat with restrictions. I realized I had some sort of compulsive binge-eating issue. I got to the point where I couldn't buy a whole pack of cookies or box of pizza because I would eat the whole thing, or at least as much as I could before I literally couldn't eat anymore. I used to have to throw food in the garbage to keep myself from overeating. That is how out of control I was. I had a bad relationship with food. I did not trust myself to be in control around it. But it was a love/hate thing.

Seven months after my college graduation I was almost 300 pounds, not quite there but the scales were tipping in that direction. That's when I linked up with my aunt to work on this book project down in South Florida. We started a diet full of fresh fruits, vegetables, lean protein, and water, and walked an hour every day. In the beginning I was out of breath and tired after walking ten minutes. But with each new day, I felt myself growing stronger and leaner. My body was so happy! I felt so clean and healthy inside, and by the end of the first week I had walked four miles! What helped me start and continue to lose weight was learning how to eat better and to exercise by actually practicing those things, not just hearing about them or thinking about them. I finally began to lose weight. The first month I lost about twelve pounds. The next month I joined a gym and I lost fifteen pounds. Then I had a pitfall because I started to get obsessed with the number on the scale. When I began cutting my calories too low, I knew that this was going to lead to me bingeing again. I decided to switch to a low-carbohydrate diet, and I have lost more than fifty pounds so far. I work well with the structure and discipline of this diet. I think that is what is important for anyone deciding to lose weight, to understand that what works for one person may not work for you. I had to find my right regimen. I continue to exercise not just to look good, but because I feel amazing as I work out. I get to bond with my exercise buddies, or when I am alone I get the chance to really think about everything going on in my life. I sleep better, I see improvements in my body, and I feel like I sweat out the stress of my day during a good workout. Sometimes I run up and down the stairs for no reason other than the fact that now I am healthy enough to do it without breaking a sweat! And now I walk up to twenty miles a day!

I am learning a lot during this process, including to pay attention to what my body is saying to me: If I am breathing too hard after walking down the block, then I need to be doing a bit more cardiovascular exercise. If I am getting full during dinner, then I put down the fork, even if there is food left on the plate. I have started to pay more attention to what I am eating and am beginning to understand which foods set me back and which give me crazy cravings. I try not to beat myself up when I stray from the way I want to eat. I just promise myself that I will do better next time. I still have seventy pounds to go. Losing those first fifty pounds has given me the confidence to continue my diet and exercise.

Having family, a boyfriend, and best friends who are so supportive of me has probably helped me the most with making changes and sticking to them. I feel like I owe it to them to be in great shape so that I can be around longer and physically keep up with them, whether we are climbing mountains or partying all night. I feel like I am beautiful no matter what I look like.

Veronica is on a mission to get healthier and leaner. I have watched her struggles with food and I know that she had to get to a place of accepting herself before she could conquer the challenge of weight loss. You can do it too. When you know that you are special and that you have value and that your life is worthwhile, then you will be in a position to overcome any obstacles in your way.

—

"You are blessed with only one body, and it is your duty to take care of it, so that it will always be able to take care of you."
–KARLA MILLS-RAYMOND (MY MOM)

You Have the Power to Redirect Your Course

In Florida, the jurisdiction of a county court judge includes handling cases involving driving under the influence (DUI). On the bench, I had a regular DUI arraignment calendar once a week that typically contained more than one hundred cases. An arraignment is a proceeding in which a person arrested or given a ticket for a criminal offense is called to court to enter a plea to the charge. One day in 2004, I was calling the arraignment calendar when a well-dressed young woman stumbled into the crowded courtroom and promptly fell flat on the floor. The entire courtroom hushed. My bailiff helped the woman to her feet, and I asked him to escort her up to the podium before me. She could barely stand on her own, and I wondered how she had made it to the courthouse, let alone to

my second-floor courtroom. She was obviously severely in-
toxicated, and it was only nine o'clock in the morning! I had
never had a defendant appear, at least not visibly, intoxi-
cated in front of me. If you are charged with DUI, the last
thing you want is for the judge to suspect that you have been
drinking before coming to court. I thought, this woman is
obviously not in her right mind. As I began trying to talk to
her, a young man walked hurriedly into the courtroom and
straight up to the podium. He identified himself as her
brother and said that the woman had not come home at all
the night before and that she was dressed in the same
clothes she had worn when he last saw her twenty-four
hours earlier. Since no sounds coming from her mouth were
making any sense to me, I immediately took a recess to ac-
cess my options. I made a few calls to alcohol rehab centers
and found one that would take her into their program immediately. Officials from the program showed up about an
hour after my call. I ordered the woman into a twenty-eight-
day residential rehab program. I let her brother know that if
she didn't go, I would take her into custody (jail, that is) for
direct contempt of court for having shown up before me
drunk. The two folks from the rehab carted her out of the
courtroom and I set a new arraignment date for a month
later, when she would appear in front of me again.

I had nearly forgotten about this woman when she
came back to court a month later escorted by counselors
from the program. She looked a lot better than she had the
last time she was in my courtroom. The counselors raved
about the great progress she had made during her time in

the program. With her head hanging in shame, she thanked me for having sent her there. She said she felt brand-new, with a brighter outlook on life. I was used to people feeling contrite and sorry after the fact; therefore, I was not impressed by anything except that she was now appearing before me *sober*. I was also a little reluctant to be completely optimistic about her acceptance of responsibility for her past transgressions. I am a big supporter of the "bring shame back" movement. There is no sense of shame or remorse these days for the wrongs that we do. Only excuses. The focus is shifted from the person with dirt on her hands to someone or something outside herself. What we do, say, and become is always someone else's fault. But she told me, "Who and what I am today is my own fault!" I told her that I put her on the road to recovery, but that only she could direct her life onto the right track and keep it there. Any and all further progress would have to depend on her. She was twenty-six with a drinking problem. She had passed out many times in bars and clubs, and often found herself inside the beds and cars of men she did not remember meeting. She told me that she had embarrassed herself and her family and that the truth was, though she had been arrested once for DUI, she had driven countless times drunk, not knowing how she got home.

There was something about her that made me believe that she was ready to change direction. I cannot put it into words. I have felt this many times in my life about people, places, and things. Call it intuition, or a gut feeling, but I believed that, if given a chance, this young woman might right her own course. With help from her public defender and the prosecutor, I offered her a deal. If she would agree to continue with the program on an outpatient basis and report her progress to me once a month for the next year, the prosecution would offer her a deal that did not include jail time. She would also have to find a job or enroll in college. She was not allowed to drive, and would have to rely on public transportation to get around. She would have no probation officer or anyone else to monitor her movements, but if she were to be arrested for any crime whatsoever, she would be immediately taken into custody and be sentenced to one year in jail. She agreed to these terms without hesitation.

Over the course of the next year, every thirty days, this woman would come to court and report to me about what she was doing. Each time, the prosecutor would run her record to make sure she had not been arrested or cited. Every report about her progress brought good news: She found a job, she cleared up her credit, she found her own apartment, she enrolled in night school, she volunteered at the rehab center to help others struggling with addiction, she was keeping a journal, and she had joined a support group for adult children of alcoholics. With every progress report, she looked better, sounded stronger, and seemed more independent. The first couple of times she showed up with counselors from the program. Eventually, she came to court on her own. There were visible signs of her life transformation in her words and appearance. After the year was completed, the prosecution closed her case. I wish I had a before-and-after picture of her so you could see the drastic change.

In 2008, the year I left the bench to start my own court show, I received a letter in my chambers. It was from that same young woman who had stumbled into my courtroom drunk four years earlier. Her case had been long lost in my mind to the thousands of cases that had come after. It was a thank-you letter. She had been sober for nearly four years. She had earned a graduate degree in childhood education and moved to Philadelphia. She was working with a pilot program to help improve the self-esteem of elementary school–age girls. She was also engaged to a man in law enforcement. She had found her own path.

It is never too late to redirect the course of our lives. Remember that we are writing our very own biographies. I have a friend, Nicole, a beautiful and vivacious woman I met at a boot camp in South Carolina during one of my many attempts to shed excess weight. During the first week of boot camp, she was always pushing me to be more active: "Come on, Karen: ten more push-ups!" "Let's take another aerobics class this afternoon!" "Hey, stop thinking about Fig Newtons!" I thought to myself, "How lucky am I to have found such a motivating friend to support my weight loss efforts." We became very close during our two weeks at boot camp. We had so much fun, and we encouraged each other to try new workouts and pushed ourselves to the limit. Near the end of boot camp, Nicole's husband and daughter drove down from Charleston to join her for dinner one night and to celebrate her birthday. I was really shocked when I met her husband. He was a much older man, by twenty years it turned out, who seemed to have a permanent frown and cloudy disposition. He was void of the personality that bubbled over from his wife, and his chair might as well have been empty. I really wanted to ask Nicole, "How did you end up marrying him?" But that was none of my business!

At the end of the boot camp we vowed to keep in touch through email and text messages. Late one night she called me sobbing, saying that her husband had slapped her and she was bleeding from her mouth. She asked me if I thought she should call the police, and I gave an emphatic "Yes!" Hesitating, she asked, "Well, what about his reputation in the community?"

Nicole and her husband were the "it" couple in their community. You know, the "power couple" who attend the high-end fund-raisers and belong to a country club. They were always throwing grand parties, organizing local events, and making large charitable contributions. I told her, "It's not your place to worry about his reputation. *He* should have thought of his reputation before he put his hands on you. If he gets away with hitting you because he knows you won't report it, then he will continue the abuse." She was also worried about her two young daughters and the impact his arrest would have on them. I told her that her girls were witnesses to the way their father was treating her, even if they were not physically in the room.

Children know more than we give them credit for. And besides, their first lessons in male-female relationships are learned through the parents' relationship. Did Nicole want her daughters growing up thinking that domestic violence is okay and that there are no repercussions? Did she want them to operate from a position of weakness in their own relationships or from a position of power?

Nicole called the police and her husband was arrested. The next day she called me back and told me what happened. I said, "Nicole, now that you've gotten me involved with your marriage, I want to ask you, how did you end up with this man?" She met him when he came to visit his family in her native country. Nicole was trying to get out of a country whose economic and social fabric had been torn apart by war and political upheaval. She saw no real future for herself there. Her future husband was well established in the United States, and he offered her a better life.

Once they married, Nicole got her college degree and eventually became a high-level manager in a company in Los Angeles. And that is when things started to go downhill in her marriage. Her husband, who had always been controlling, felt threatened by her success and the fact that she was working around a lot of men. He intimidated her into quitting her job and then moved them all the way across the country to the much smaller community of Charleston, South Carolina. That is when she became a housewife and mother for twenty years. Because she wanted to be a good wife and mother, she became totally submissive to her husband's wants and demands. It was hard for me to imagine what it must have been like for her to deny her own identity for two decades for the sake of someone else. To me, it would be like asking a peacock not to spread its plumes! She recounted to me the abusive treatment she had endured during that time: He beat her, slapped her, threw her down in a hotel room, threatened to burn her clothes—all kinds of horrible things. After years of this abuse, she said, "I've had enough."

Nicole relied on her friends and family for moral support as she began to disentangle her life from that of her husband's. She'd been with this man since she was a teenager. She had not been in the driver's seat of her own life for two decades. She was scared to take the steps to leave her husband and to establish a life on her own. During this difficult transition, one of Nicole's friends was hell-bent on convincing her to stay in the marriage. She told Nicole she was acting selfishly if she divorced her husband and would bring shame on her family and on her children. Every time Nicole spoke to this woman, she would end up questioning whether she was making the right decision about the divorce, and she would be set back a few paces in her resolve to end things.

Nicole finally gathered the courage to break the news to her daughters and was surprised when both of her girls said they knew what was going on all along. "We saw how controlling Daddy was and how unhappy he made you. You are a lot happier now that he has moved out and we are happier too because it doesn't feel uneasy in the house anymore." The thing she feared the most, disappointing her daughters, was nothing to fear at all. The divorce is final, and Nicole is going back to school to get her master's degree. She is also working again in her profession, which she had missed so much. I spoke to her on the phone the other day and told her that I was writing about her struggle and triumph in my book. Her exact words were, "I am just a work in progress and I am loving this journey so much! At times it feels like I am moving a piano by myself, slipping and struggling, but at the end of the day, I fall asleep with a big smile on my face. I am finally in control of my life!"

I know, without a doubt, that you can take control over the direction your life is going. My own life has veered off track enough times for me to know that you can always get yourself back on track. Whether it is disentangling your life from someone who is abusive or freeing yourself from an addiction, you *can* free yourself. The key is in surrounding yourself with people who support your growth and who cheer you on. Anybody in your life who is not on the cheering squad needs to be booted out! Remember, you're the captain of your own team!

⊢

"Security is mostly a superstition. It does not exist in nature, nor do the children of men as a whole experience it. Avoiding danger is no safer in the long run than outright exposure. Life is either a daring adventure, or nothing!"
—HELEN KELLER

You Can Be a Renaissance Woman Too

When I was in law school I met a woman named Ava Parker who would eventually become one of my very best friends. We would greet each other when we saw each other around campus, but we weren't friends. Two years later on my first job as a lawyer at the Dade County Public Defender's Office, I met Ava again. She had moved down from a little town called Milton, Florida. Never heard of it? Neither had I. She had accepted a job in the public defender's office also. We became immediate friends. Ava and I tried many cases together. We loved trial work, and became strong advocates for our clients. After a few years practicing law in Miami, Ava moved on to bigger things, working on state projects in the capital. But we always stayed in touch and saw each other regularly.

One day Ava called me and said, "Karen, my daddy died last week." But before I could absorb that, she said, "And Mommy died this morning." I fell into my chair, and we both started crying. For the next few minutes, all I could repeat through my tears was, "Oh, no." Finally I said, "Ava, I'm coming right up to Milton." I dropped what I was doing that moment, got a ticket to North Florida, and was there the next morning. When I was trying to make travel arrangements to get to Milton, I called the home of Ava's parents, and her older sister answered. She said, "I don't know why you are bothering to come up here. Ava has a husband." She meant well, but I knew that husbands and boyfriends can come and go, but good friends are forever. So I told her, "I'm coming anyway."

When I landed in Pensacola, I picked up a rental car for the drive to Milton. When I pulled into town, Ava said she was in a department store picking out clothes in which to dress her mother. I pulled into the shopping complex and went inside the store to find her. I spotted Ava in the shoe department with her sister-in-law, and her face was stoic. She looked okay, like she was handling the situation better than could be expected. I breathed a sigh of relief. As she looked up, we locked eyes and we both burst into tears. We ended up on the floor sobbing. Her sister-in-law said, "She's been holding it together all day, but when she saw you it was over!" I knew I had done the right thing by coming.

Many family members and friends came to pay their respects to Ava's mother, Mrs. Nellie Parker. As her procession moved through the streets of this small panhandle town, traffic pulled over to the side of the road. People on the sidewalk stopped and bowed their heads. I had never witnessed this type of respect for a funeral procession and for the departed person. There had to be well over four hundred people in the church. There was not one empty seat. And some of these people had said good-bye to Mr. Parker less than a week earlier. The two had been married more than half a century. There was a procession of people who spoke at the funeral, but there were two eulogists that really struck me. One was a man in his forties who got up and told us that Mrs. Parker had been his seventh-grade teacher, and she had been his motivation to make something of himself in this life. She had written a song for her students to encourage them to excel in mathematics called, "Math is Important." He then called up about ten other people who had been his classmates some thirty-odd years ago and they all sang the song from memory! It brought the church to tears.

The other memorable speaker was her brother-in-law. He told us about her extraordinary life. She was born in Defuniak Springs, Florida, in 1925, and she was determined to have an education at a time when black women from small southern towns couldn't even try on clothes in department stores, let alone hope for a meaningful career. She earned her degree in mathematics at Florida A&M University and later taught math in a small town outside of Tallahassee. She moved to Milton in the 1960s. It was while teaching in

Milton that Mrs. Parker realized how many black children had no idea how to formulate a plan for a successful career after high school. She decided that her skills could best be used to better her students if she got a master's degree in counseling. So she went back to college while raising four school-aged children of her own. Once she earned her degree, she became a guidance counselor at the high school. Some of those students were at the funeral too. Mrs. Parker believed that a person should be diverse and learned in many areas of their life. She was an artist who painted watercolors, a musician who played the piano and wrote many songs, and a community leader. She had card parties, exercised daily, and prayed.

Her brother-in-law told us that Mrs. Parker believed that a life should be as full as possible. And she was already a complete person when she decided to enrich her life even further by going into the ministry. She was one of the first female ministers in the African Methodist Church and endured a lot of sexism and strife because people felt like a woman shouldn't be in her position. Her brother-in-law ended his eulogy by telling us that "Nellie Parker was a renaissance woman." The words struck me like lightning! I thought about what it meant to be a renaissance woman: a person who sets her own agenda for her achievements and the direction her life will take. I heard someone else define a "renaissance woman" as a winner not a whiner, a leader not a follower, a victor not a victim. After the funeral when I saw Ava back at the house for the repast, I said: "Ava, we should dry our tears. Your mother lived a life by her own terms and convictions. Through her life story, there are many lessons we can learn about our own paths. She left us with a powerful legacy. We are going to be renaissance women too!" I made the decision then and there that I was going to live my life like Nellie Parker. I want to continue to write and rewrite my own biography. And at the end of *my* life I want people to get up at my funeral and say all the things that I have done to help people, to make a difference, to enrich my life, and to make my time on earth worthwhile and memorable.

We can all learn lessons from Mrs. Parker's journey. She epitomized what it means to live your best life. She never stopped growing in her desire to test the limits of her mind and creative energy. She was vigilant in her search for avenues to make her good better and her better best. And she did it all by maneuvering around the roadblocks and pitfalls laid out by a society determined to impede her journey. She stayed in her lane and true to the path her heart led her to take. Her story made me want to be a renaissance woman. Her story still inspires me today to keep learning, to keep loving, and to keep growing. I hope you too have been inspired to direct your path down the best road that life offers. The road of possibilities.

├─

"How long after you are gone will ripples remain as evidence that you were cast into the pool of life?"
—Grant M. Bright

Fasten Your Seat Belts!

I hope that, through my experiences and insights, you have been inspired to really pause and think about where you are in your own life. Everything that I have written about here has involved some facet of my own story. I have given you details of my journey that informed my choices and continue to shape the person that I am and the path that I am taking.

I am not the same person I was twenty years ago, or ten years ago for that matter. I am even further along in my growth and awareness than I was 365 days ago. We are all on a journey with opportunities for revelation, discovery, and real growth. I hope that by reading this book you have been inspired to point your life in the direction you want to go. Life is like driving down a never-ending highway, and our paths will at times be peppered with unexpected challenges such as accidents and traffic jams. How we live our best life depends on how we react to those challenges. I have always refused to be a victim. There is no power or glory in it. And when there is a choice between darkness and the light, I will always choose the light and hope you will too. I encourage you to be positive and courageous as you navigate the curves and negotiate any hazards you may encounter along the way.

Now check your mirrors, fasten your seat belts, and start your engines. Have fun along the journey and always remember to STAY IN YOUR LANE!

About the Author

JUDGE KAREN MILLS-FRANCIS is the star of TV's syndicated shows *Judge Karen* and *Judge Karen's Court*. She was born and raised in Miami, Florida, the oldest of five children. She practiced criminal defense law for thirteen years, both in private practice and as a public defender, and was elected twice as Miami-Dade County Court judge, only the second African American woman ever to serve in that position. She is a respected advocate for disadvantaged youth and victims of domestic violence, and often speaks around the country on these issues. She is currently developing and designing a line of shapewear and swimsuits for curvy women. Judge Karen Mills-Francis is a graduate of Bowdoin College and Levin School of Law at the University of Florida.

www.myjudgeKaren.com

About the Type

This book was set in Caslon, a typeface first designed in 1722 by William Caslon. Its widespread use by most English printers in the early eighteenth century soon supplanted the Dutch typefaces that had formerly prevailed. The roman is considered a "workhorse" typeface due to its pleasant, open appearance, while the italic is exceedingly decorative.